Win the Talent Game

WIN *the* TALENT GAME

A GUIDE TO LATERAL HIRING
FOR LAW FIRMS AND LAWYERS

RICHARD BROCK

HOUNDSTOOTH
PRESS

WIN THE TALENT GAME
A Guide to Lateral Hiring for Law Firms and Lawyers

FIRST EDITION

ISBN 978-1-5445-4418-2 *Hardcover*
978-1-5445-4416-8 *Paperback*
978-1-5445-4417-5 *Ebook*

This book is dedicated to my two favorite lawyers:

To my late father, Paul W. Brock, Sr. He loved being a lawyer.

To my wife, Heather. For everything.

CONTENTS

SECTION IV: COMMON MISTAKES BY LAW FIRMS AND LATERALS

SECTION V: SPECIAL CONSIDERATIONS IN LATERAL HIRING

AUTHOR'S NOTES

THE LAWYERS AND LAW FIRMS COVERED IN THIS BOOK
are those serving the corporate community. These firms range
in size from the largest firms in the world to sole practitioners,
and their clients are businesses, financial institutions, healthcare
providers, insurance companies, and similar entities. I am not
referring to lawyers or firms that typically represent individuals.
Lawyers who practice Family Law, Criminal Law, Personal
Injury Law, Disability Law, individual Debtor Bankruptcy, and
similar practices that typically serve individuals (as opposed to
business entities) usually have a different business model and
are not the subject of this book.

Furthermore, from this point on, "laterals" in this book will
mean partner-level lawyers who have moved or are considering
moving from one law firm to another. This is distinguished
from associate-level lawyers and any lawyers who are moving
in-house, into a government position, or into a position outside
of the law.

Finally, throughout the book, I use the term "partners" to
include all lawyers who have achieved the status of partner,

shareholder, member, owner, officer, and so on. This includes both equity and non-equity partners.

INTRODUCTION

THERE ARE ALWAYS WINNERS AND LOSERS

IN SO MANY HUMAN ENDEAVORS, RANGING FROM CHIL-
dren's games on the playground to wars between nations, there
are winners and losers.

In the legal industry, the winners and losers can be seen in
the trajectory and status of law firms. Why do some law firms
seem to do so much better than others? Why do some firms
seem to always grow, represent the best clients, and make the
most money? Conversely, why do some previously successful
firms seem to be stagnant, or shrinking, or even irrelevant?

In a word, *talent*. Talent is the foundation of all businesses,
including law firms. The law firms that win are the ones that
have the most talent and have implemented the cultures and
systems to effectively support that talent.

This, of course, raises the question: if talent will put law firms
in the winner's circle, how do the firms acquire it?

The answer is *lateral hiring*. The law firms that are winning in
the 21st Century are the ones that are the best at lateral hiring.

These firms acquire the most talent, which brings in the best clients and generates the highest compensation.

If you are a law firm leader, you may be thinking to yourself, "That is all well and good, but *how* do we become the best at lateral hiring? For that matter, how do we just get better at lateral hiring?"

If you are a lawyer considering a lateral move, how do you do it the right way? What issues do you need to consider, and what questions do you need to ask?

Consider two similar law firms based in the same market. They are approximately the same size, each with about 200 lawyers. Both are considered regional law firms, with 90 lawyers in their founding office and three smaller offices in nearby states. They have similar profits per equity partner (PEPs) and revenues per lawyer (RPLs), and total revenues of between $140 million and $160 million. Both have excellent lawyers with good clients. Neither firm has significant debt or collection issues. Both are interested in growing or, at a minimum, sustaining their current level of success.

In seven years, however, we will revisit them and see that one of these firms, Firm A, is thriving. It has grown by over 30 percent in both headcount and revenue. It now has 260 lawyers. RPL is up, and total firm revenues have grown to over $200 million. Bill rates have significantly increased. PEPs have increased by nearly 20 percent. New clients have been added. Offices in two additional cities have opened, and new practice areas are being offered to current and prospective clients. Most significantly, all of these improvements have created even more opportunities for the future.

The other firm, Firm B, has not fared so well. Firm B has shrunk by one-third and now has 135 lawyers. Some lawyers retired, and others made lateral moves to other firms. Some made lateral moves to Firm A because the future seems so much brighter at Firm A. With lower headcount, of course, comes lower firm revenues and lower RPLs. Most unfortunately, Firm B's PEPs are down significantly, over 25 percent, which means the remaining partners at Firm B are, on average, bringing home much less money than they did previously. The trends are discouraging. Every week it seems like another partner announces he is leaving to join another firm. The best clients are sending less work, and few new clients are retaining Firm B to handle their legal work.

Needless to say, any law firm leader or practicing lawyer wants to make sure they follow the path of Firm A. No one wants to be in Firm B, even though there are quite a few law firms that look like Firm B today. So how does a law firm leader accomplish this? How does she make sure her firm experiences growth, success, better clients, and higher incomes? How does a practicing lawyer make sure he joins a firm like Firm A?

To answer these questions and many related ones, I wrote this book.

I have been working with law firms and lateral attorneys for over 25 years, and before that, I spent nearly five years practicing commercial litigation. I have had the privilege of working as a consultant, recruiter, career coach, and strategic advisor for law firms, lawyers, and corporate legal departments throughout the country. During this time, I have been fortunate to have successfully placed hundreds of lateral attorneys, and facilitated dozens of law firm mergers and practice group acquisitions, with some of the best law firms in America.

Experience has shown me the vital importance of lateral hiring for healthy law firms, and it has taught me to identify certain patterns that usually lead to success (or failure) in a firm's lateral hiring efforts. Similarly, I have learned the motivations and concerns most prospective laterals have when considering changing law firms, and I have learned the pitfalls laterals should avoid in order to achieve a successful lateral move.

My goal is for this book to serve as an effective guideline for both law firms and lateral attorneys as they navigate the lateral hiring landscape. I want this book to improve law firms' lateral hiring processes and help them produce better talent acquisition results. I also want this book to help laterals land in law firms that advance their careers and increase their job satisfaction. In short, and circling back to our example above, I wrote this book so that more law firms and laterals end up with a law firm and career like those found in Firm A.

SECTION

The Legal Talent Market: An Overview

CHAPTER 1

IT'S THE JIMMIES AND JOES

I AM A COLLEGE FOOTBALL FAN. I DO NOT REALLY KNOW why. Ever since I was a kid, I have absolutely loved college football (along with college basketball). When I played games as a kid, I would often pretend I scored the game-winning touchdown in the Sugar Bowl or the big rivalry game. For whatever reason, the college game has always fascinated me.

I loved (and still love) the pageantry, the marching bands, the campuses, the students, the cheerleaders, and everything else about the college football game. Of course, I realize the college game is far from the "pure amateur" endeavor it may have been at one time. It is a multibillion-dollar business at the highest levels, and certainly there are negative elements of big-time college football. But the emotions, passion, and excitement continue to appeal to me as a fan—and are what I believe differentiate the college game from the pro game.

A less obvious but significant difference between college football and pro football is the structure for acquiring talent.

Professional football is, at least in theory, designed to have parity throughout the leagues. The theory is that if the teams have roughly equal talent, then the games will be more competitive and interesting, and a greater number of teams will have success and win championships over a number of years.

To achieve parity, professional sports leagues impose specific rules about talent acquisition. In some pro sports leagues, such as the NFL, the teams that have the worst records usually are given higher draft picks, meaning they have the first shot at the most talented players. The NFL wants the worst teams to sign the best, most talented players coming out of college so that their teams improve. Thus, parity is achieved.

Yet, in college sports, the system of talent acquisition is very different. Instead of giving weaker teams a better shot at players to recruit from, in college sports each team has an equal chance to recruit whoever they want to join. If a team determines they need a quarterback and three offensive linemen, they go out and try to locate the very best ones around. Then they try to recruit that quarterback and those offensive linemen to come play for their school. It works the same way in basketball, gymnastics, softball, and every other college sport.

In other words, in college athletics, when you need talent for your team, there is no league to regulate your choices. You just go out and try to get the best talent you can through deliberate and persistent recruiting efforts. It is said that recruiting is the lifeblood of college sports. This is true. If you want to win, you find the best talent and then recruit that talent to come play for your team.

Of course, to be consistently successful at the highest level, you must have more than talent. You have to have good coaching, proper conditioning and nutrition, a good strategy, and in-game tactics. All of these factors and many others make the difference between a Top 5 program and an also-ran.

Above all else, if you want to win big in college sports, you need elite talent. You need the players. If my favorite team (the University of Alabama) has better players than its opponents, then my team is going to win the vast majority of games. No matter how well the opposing team is coached, and no matter how hard its players try, if my team has better players, then my team is usually going to win.

An old saying in college football sums it up: It's not the X's and O's; it's the Jimmies and Joes. If the players (Jimmy, Joe, etc.) on my team are bigger, stronger, faster, and tougher than the players on your team, then my team is probably going to win. Your team may have a better coach and coaching staff—a group that excels at the X's and O's. But if the talent disparity is great enough, it probably will not matter. My team will win because of the difference in talent.

What does all of this have to do with talent in the legal industry? As an analogy, college football is remarkably similar to the legal industry. Just as in college sports, the overriding difference between a winning and losing law firm is talent. There is constant, daily competition between law firms and between lawyers, and the winners inevitably are those with the most talent.

Of course, law firms do not play actual games with scores that reveal a winner and a loser of the contest (trials notwithstanding). However, law firms compete every single day, and every lawyer in private practice can attest to the competition he or she constantly feels. Lawyers and law firms compete primarily for clients, of course, but they also compete fiercely for talent. Or at least, the wisest law firms compete fiercely for talent.

This talent comes in the form of law students, lateral associates, and those with the most value to law firms: lateral partners with portable books of business. And, just as in college football, the law firms that have the most talent usually win. They land the best clients, hire the brightest law students, add the most valuable laterals, and, ultimately, make the most money.

It becomes a cycle. The best lawyers want to practice with the best firms because those are the firms that provide the highest compensation and the most interesting and sophisticated work. When the best lawyers join those firms, they strengthen them, thereby enabling these firms to provide even higher compensation and even more interesting and sophisticated work. This, of course, attracts other top lawyers, and the cycle repeats itself.

The difference between winning and losing in college football is the Jimmies and Joes. In the legal industry, the difference between winning and losing is the Jennies and Joes. The principle is the same.

CHAPTER 2

WHAT IS TALENT?

TALENT IS ONE OF THOSE UBIQUITOUS WORDS. WE SEE IT used in many different contexts to describe many different types of people. Often, we think of the rich and famous as the ones who have talent. William Shakespeare had talent. Jim Thorpe had talent. Aretha Franklin had talent.

And, of course, this is all true. Those famous people certainly had talent, and quite a bit of it.

However, talent is not limited to the rich and famous. Nor is talent limited to abilities one is born with. Talent includes abilities that are developed through years of practice. This willingness to put in the hard work, this diligence, this perseverance, this work ethic: all are part of what we mean by talent.

Take two musicians of roughly equal ability. Tom likes to play the guitar, but he also has other interests. He will pick up his guitar a few times per week, strum on it a bit, and play a few chords, but that is about it as far as devoting time to the instrument.

Jerry, on the other hand, is dedicated to making himself a great guitar player. He practices for a minimum of one hour per day, although he often plays for two to three hours. Playing the guitar is a central component of his life, and every year he gets better and better at his instrument.

Who has more talent? Some might say they have equal talent, and that Jerry has simply done a better job of developing his talent. I submit that Jerry has more talent because he has been more dedicated to developing his innate abilities. Jerry's commitment and diligence are a major part of his talent, and therefore he is clearly the most talented.

In the legal industry, talent is multifaceted. It is not just about innate skills and intelligence. And it is more than the ability to do the tasks a lawyer must perform in his or her practice. It also includes other critical facets.

First and foremost, the ability to bring in clients is a crucial talent. In fact, for lawyers in private practice, this may be the most important talent they can possess. A lawyer can be the most technically brilliant practitioner in the world, but if he does not have any clients, his brilliance is worthless.

Additionally, a lawyer must have talent for communicating with other people, whether clients, judges, opposing counsel, juries, law partners, bosses, or staff members. The ability to effectively communicate with varying groups of people is definitely a talent.

The willingness and ability to work hard is also a talent. It is indisputable that the lawyer who puts in extra effort, bills more hours, and outworks the competition possesses an additional type of talent. Her work ethic, her willingness to capitalize on her drive, is itself a huge talent.

Finally, one could say that experience is a major component of what we mean by talent in the legal industry. Or more accurately, experience is an enhancer of talent. Compare two attorneys who have similar IQs as well as communication and people skills. Both are litigators. One is a third-year associate. The other has 20 years of experience in litigation. Who has the most talent?

Some would say their talent levels are equal, and the level of experience is a separate question. But when it comes to the legal industry, I disagree. In this arena, I believe the definition of talent includes not just innate abilities but also experience, personal skills, communication skills, management skills, leadership skills, business development skills, work ethic, and other factors. To put it another way, for those of us who work in and around the legal industry, "talent" means a lawyer's overall value in the market. This sentence should be repeated because it is a core principle of this book: *talent means a lawyer's overall value in the market.*

The lawyers who are most in demand in the private sector are those with the most inherent value in the market. In other words, the lawyers who are most in demand are those with the most talent.

CHAPTER 3

_____

A BRIEF HISTORY
OF LAW FIRMS

NEARLY ALL LAW FIRMS OF ANY SIZE THAT SERVE COR-
porate America are interested in hiring lateral partners. The
reasons for this desire to add laterals will be discussed in Chapter 5. But for now, it is important to simply recognize this desire
as a fact of law firm life.

Interestingly, the prevalence of law firms growing through
lateral hiring is a relatively new phenomenon. As recently as
the 1980s, few firms engaged in lateral hiring as a strategy. It
would happen occasionally, but it was still a relatively uncommon occurrence.

Up until this time, law firms were typically much smaller
and more regional. What happened to change the dynamic?
Why has lateral hiring become such a big deal over the past
few decades?

There are several reasons. First, law firms began to consoli-
date. This led to regional, national, and international law firms.
Clients liked the idea of using one law firm for various legal

issues in multiple cities wherever they had needs. These large entities had more resources and expertise to offer clients, and accordingly, they became more attractive to other lawyers as a place to practice.

Second, law firms became more business oriented. For decades, there had been tension in the legal industry about whether the law was a profession or a business. Law firms were always businesses, of course, but lawyers did not consider themselves businessmen and businesswomen. Today, however, many attorneys *do* view themselves as business professionals whose service just happens to be the law. That is a significant shift in perspective.

Third, clients changed their views on outside counsel. They became more loyal to individual lawyers as opposed to the actual law firms. This made the individual lawyers much more mobile, if they so desired.

Yet the most likely reason lateral hiring became such a central part of the legal industry, and the world of law firms, is that the economic model changed. Again, up until the 1980s, the vast majority of law firms were lockstep. Today, only a minority of firms still utilize a lockstep compensation model.

I will explain. During the 1980s/1990s, lawyers became increasingly disenchanted with the fact that some of them were generating much more revenue than their partners but were paid less simply due to the number of years they had been at the firm. Despite tradition and precedent, they viewed this as extremely unfair.

These dissatisfied lawyers would complain to their current firms. Usually, this got them nowhere, so they eventually began considering other options. This typically meant starting their own merit-based firms or moving to another law firm that would pay them large bonuses based on production. Believe it or not, seeking primarily merit-based compensation was a somewhat radical concept among lawyers as recently as the 1980s.

Before long, productive lawyers all across the country became interested in these merit-based compensation models. They believed that if they were the most productive and profitable lawyers at their firms, then they should receive the highest compensation no matter their age or the number of years they had been working there.

This new model has dramatically changed the way lawyers have viewed themselves over the past 30-plus years. Up until the 1980s, the vast majority of lawyers never changed firms. A typical career path went like this: Lawyer A graduated from law school. He may or may not have a judicial clerkship. He worked as an associate for six to seven years, made partner, and worked as a partner for approximately 35 to 40 years. Finally, he retired. (Back then, most law firms had only partners and associates, with perhaps a few lawyers who were Of Counsel. It was unusual to have non-equity partners or income partners.)

Certainly, there were exceptions to the typical career path. Some lawyers became judges, and others went into politics. A few would go into business or become in-house counsel. A few might change law firms, but that was fairly unusual.

As a part of this pattern, most lawyers were incredibly loyal to their firms. After all, they were closely tied to their employers for their entire careers. Most firms were much smaller back then, which meant most lawyers knew their law partners personally. Their law partners felt like true business partners. It was not just a legal title, but meant something on a fundamental level.

Furthermore, the lockstep compensation system promoted this sense of partnership. Lawyers did not really compete with their colleagues because the compensation structure was locked in. If Bob and Jane graduated in the same law school class and entered the firm at the same time, then Bob and Jane were going to make the same amount of money for the duration of their careers, absent some extraordinary situation.

This meant Bob and Jane did not compete, because there was really no reason to compete. If they did good work when they were associates, then they would both be made partner. Tracking originations was not really a major point of emphasis because, again, this did not impact compensation, so there was little point in emphasizing it. If Jane was a good rainmaker bringing in a lot of business, and Bob was a great brief writer who brought in very little business, that was fine because, to the firm, their value was comparable. Perhaps not equal, but comparable. Pursuant to the lockstep compensation system, they were paid the same amount of money. Bob and Jane both felt significant loyalty to their firm.

But things began to change when firms shifted away from a lockstep model and toward more of a merit-based compensation model. Now, they would each be paid a different amount based on their value to the firm.

Jane realized she was bringing in a lot more business than Bob. If not for her (and others like her), Bob would not have any work to do, period. Why should they be paid the same when she created much more value for her firm?

Bob, of course, saw things differently. In Bob's mind, he was the backbone of the law firm. Bringing in the work was great, but someone had to actually do the work. The briefs had to be written. Jane was certainly not going to do it. Between her business trips and community activities, she would never get the briefs written. Plus, Bob billed more hours than Jane anyway. In his mind, he should make just as much as, if not more money than, Jane.

These diverging viewpoints weakened the feeling between

Bob and Jane that they were truly business partners. Now, they were competitors in a contest to earn the most money out of a finite account. After all, there is only so much cash to be distributed among a partnership, and it is a zero-sum game. Bob and Jane did still share the same point of view about one thing: more money for one of them meant less money for the other.

These scenarios played out in law firms all across the country. Lawyers began to feel increasingly disgruntled with their compensation compared to their colleagues'. The lawyers who brought in clients, the rainmakers (Jane in the above example), demanded greater compensation because they were providing the revenue stream. The service partners, or those whose main contribution was performing the bulk of the legal work (Bob in the above example), demanded at least equal compensation because they were providing the service being paid for.

This put firm management in a difficult spot. Law firm leaders across the country responded in a number of different ways. Some tried to maintain the status quo and continue with the lockstep system. As noted previously, these firms do still exist today, but they are in the minority.

Other firms adjusted their compensation to varying degrees. Some maintained their basic compensation model but implemented bonuses for rainmakers and top producers. Other firms were more aggressive and completely overhauled their lockstep compensation system. These firms became true meritocracies in which the rainmakers and top producers began to be paid significantly more than the service attorneys.

The firms that moved more slowly, and either did not change their compensation systems or changed them more gradually and cautiously, often ended up in a worse position. Some of these firms began a slow decline and ultimately were absorbed by a stronger competitor through a law firm acquisition. Others shrank to a smaller size, and have remained smaller and some-what stagnant for several decades. Some have been able to maintain their size and headcount, but their competitor firms grew substantially and are now much larger with deeper bench strength and resources.

What does this broad change in compensation have to do with lateral hiring? Everything. Under a merit-based compensation system, law firms now needed the most productive, profitable attorneys available in order for their firms to thrive. Of course, law firms needed productive lawyers under the old lockstep model too but focused primarily on improving their *existing* lawyers.

Under the merit-based model, law firms concluded that the best way to get productive lawyers is to *recruit them from other firms*. Productive lawyers realized they could make a lot more money if they moved to a firm that offered a merit-based compensation system. And so they did, in ever-increasing numbers.

This change in approach has led to the rapid growth of lateral attorney hiring, which in turn has led to larger and larger law firms, along with the prevailing view of the law as a business as opposed to a profession. In fact, some law firms are *really* huge businesses. More than 50 firms generated over $1 billion in gross revenues in the 2023 AmLaw rankings. A law firm of that size would have been unthinkable only a few decades ago.

THE LAW FIRM HIERARCHY

Let's recap how the shift in compensation model has affected the hierarchy of lawyers within firms.

In the law firm market today, the most valuable players are the rainmakers like Jane, the lawyers who bring clients and business (i.e., revenue) in the door. After all, it does not matter how great of a lawyer someone is or how superior his or her legal skills are if there are no clients to serve. The market has decided that those who bring in business are more valuable than those who service the clients.

This distinction assumes the rainmaker, Jane, and the service lawyer, Bob, are two different people. Often, the rainmaker is also a high-producing working attorney. This, of course, is the ideal lawyer for a firm. Every firm wants the lawyer who is a great rainmaker, a hard worker who bills many hours, and an elite attorney with superior legal skills. Those lawyers exist, but not in abundance. The distinction makes more sense when we view the rainmaker and the service partner as two different people.

The firms that were slower to change began to decline because they did not adapt to market conditions. They did not make the internal adjustments needed to retain their most valuable assets. The rainmakers began to leave, making *lateral moves* to the firms that had made changes in response to the market. These rainmakers realized their value and capitalized on this by moving to firms that recognized their value and compensated them accordingly.

The firms to which these rainmakers moved became stronger. Their revenues went up. Their business increased. Now they could hire additional attorneys to work as service partners to handle the business the rainmakers were bringing in.

As a consequence of the market's revised consideration of value, the service partners were now viewed differently. They now had less equity than the rainmakers and, in some cases, were no longer equity partners. Around this time, many law firms created the two-tiered partnership model. The firms created "equity" and "non-equity" partners, or "equity" and "income" partners. As the name implies, equity partners are those who own equity in the firm. They are the actual firm owners. Income partners or non-equity partners do not have ownership in the firm, but they retain the title of "partner" to help with client relations and as a sign of respect for their experience level and contributions to the firm.

The two-tiered partnership model was created for several reasons, one of which was to improve reported performance metrics such as the PEPs (profits per equity partner) formerly PPP (profits per partner). Another reason was to further distinguish between those who generated business and those who did not. If a lawyer wanted to "make equity," she had to get out there and bring in enough business to justify it.

In the end, the new law firm hierarchy solidified. The rainmakers won and the service partners lost. Those are the market dynamics at work. It is hard, however, to not sympathize with the service partners. They held up their end of the deal. When they began practicing law, they were told that if they did good work and billed enough hours, they would make partner. Afterward, as long as they continued to work hard and produce quality legal work, they would remain partners and earn a good living, and that would be that.

But the deal changed for them. Now they were expected to generate business, or firms would shunt them to a lower rung of the hierarchy. Many of them, though, were not particularly suited to business development. Others simply did not want to. Some service partners began to say things such as "I did not go to law school to be a salesperson." On at least one level, they were correct: business development *is* sales. Lawyers may not like thinking of business development this way, but that is exactly what it is.

Regardless, some service partners' inability or unwillingness to go out and bring in clients (i.e., to sell) only made the situation worse for them. They thought it was unfair, and maybe you do too. But ask yourself these questions: Are teachers not more valuable to society than actors? Are firefighters not more valuable to the community than professional athletes? According to the market, the answer to both questions is clearly no. The market is not emotional. The market does not care who wins and who loses. But the market rules, and it has made its ruling in the legal industry. Rainmakers are more valuable than service partners. Period.

The market shows us this in several different ways. First and foremost, as I have explained, the rainmakers are usually the highest-paid lawyers within law firms. Depending on a firm's compensation structure, it is the rainmakers who receive the most points and/or the highest draw. They also receive the largest distributions and/or the largest bonuses, whether formulaic or discretionary. And, of course, they are given more resources with which to speak, travel, wine, dine, and ultimately bring in more clients.

Perhaps most importantly, rainmakers are the ones retained when economic downturns occur. In such times, their value becomes more apparent than ever. This all makes sense: when revenues shrink, those who bring revenue in the door ascend to an even higher status within the firm, and the importance of retaining them becomes more pronounced. One of the ways in which firms ensure the retention of the rainmakers during down periods is by *increasing* their compensation, even when firm revenue is decreasing.

How do firms accomplish this? They look for numerous ways to decrease expenses, of course, which includes de-equitizing and sometimes expelling service partners from the firm. Sometimes firms crunch the numbers and conclude the only way to pay Rainmaker A enough money to ensure she will stay with the firm is by removing Service Partner B from the firm. Not only are service partners paid less—often much less—but they are also sometimes in danger of being removed from the firm entirely during inevitable economic downturns.

CHAPTER 4

FINDERS, MINDERS, AND GRINDERS

IN CHAPTER 3, WE DISCUSSED HOW THE MARKET DETER-mined that not all law firm partners are created equal. Although this was not always the case, it certainly is today. To summarize the hierarchy within most modern law firms, someone coined the phrase "finders, minders, and grinders."

Finders, as the name implies, are the ones who go out and find the business. They bring clients in the door. These are the rainmakers, and the market has placed them at the top of the pyramid.

Below the finders are the minders. These are the lawyers responsible for maintaining client relationships. The minders oversee the work that is being done on a given matter, and they often have billing responsibility to make sure the clients are billed fairly and efficiently, so that the client relationship remains strong and profitable.

Finally, below the minders are the grinders. These are the lawyers who actually do the bulk of the legal work. They are researching the issues, writing the briefs, taking at least some of the depositions, and drafting the deal documents. All associates will spend time as grinders, of course, and sometimes lawyers who are not interested in being a partner will gladly assume a grinder's role.

At the partner level, the lawyers within law firms who are mainly grinders are, of course, the service partners. There are definite positives to working as a service partner/grinder within a good law firm. You get to do high-end legal work. You probably work on some very interesting matters. You spend your time practicing law as opposed to developing business.

The biggest drawback to working as a service partner/ grinder within a good law firm is that you are dependent on other lawyers to provide work for you to do. Your ability to generate revenue depends on others' ability and willingness to give you work. That is a highly vulnerable position, especially during a downturn.

By contrast, the finder is not only in the best position in her law firm, but she is also in one of the best positions in the entire workforce. A lawyer in private practice with a client base has a tremendous amount of control over her career. To start, there are literally hundreds of private practice areas that she can pursue as her chosen career path. Then, upon choosing a particular practice area, she has the ability to go out and generate as much business as she is capable of generating, giving her a significant amount of control over her work on a daily basis.

Lawyers in private practice also have the ability to change employers almost whenever they want, provided the market is there for lawyers with their background. There are essentially no non-compete restrictions on lawyers, which further enables them to move around at their discretion.

All of this gives the lawyer in private practice a level of

autonomy and economic security far greater than that of professionals in most industries. But this is only possible if they have their own client base. Without clients, or a "portable book of business," as it is known, lawyers are usually not able to change firms when they want to. This makes the grinders even more dependent. Not only do they rely on finders for work, but also when they have issues or problems with their firm, it is very difficult for them to leave.

For this reason, if you are reading this as a lawyer, I strongly advise you to get out and develop your own client base. I realize that does not happen overnight, but the sooner you start doing this, the better. In my experience, developing a client base is by far the most important step any lawyer in private practice can take in order to advance his or her career. It is particularly true if you are a young lawyer, although it is applicable to lawyers at all levels of experience.

Let me give you an example of how this might look in your day-to-day life, especially if you are a young lawyer. If it is late one evening, and you have decided to work for one more hour before going home, then you should spend that hour on business development rather than billing that hour, absent a deadline or another urgent situation. Many law firms would disagree. In the short term, it is in the law firm's best interest for you to bill another hour. However, for your career advancement, the best way for you to spend that hour is by trying to bring in business, or by learning how.

Some lawyers do not like this advice either. As mentioned earlier, I have had numerous attorneys tell me things such as "I did not go to law school to be a salesperson." While I understand the sentiment, I can tell you that is a very shortsighted view of today's legal industry. Back in the 1980s, a lawyer could probably hold that perspective and still have a successful legal career. But in today's legal market, although it may not be impossible, it will be much more difficult to eschew business development and still achieve career success in private practice.

You may ask, "What is so wrong with wanting to be a grinder or maybe a minder but not a finder?" There is nothing wrong per se with that point of view. The problem, as we have seen, is that it is the finders who have the most value in the market, the most career autonomy and security, and the highest compensation within law firms. So, while it may be true that a lawyer did not go to law school in order to be a salesperson, the wisest lawyers quickly realize that sales (i.e., business development) is an essential part of career success. In fact, I would argue that it is the single most important part of career success for a lawyer in private practice, assuming reasonably strong legal skills.

Being a good lawyer is obviously essential, but it is really just the minimum threshold. Unless you are truly exceptional and/or have a unique niche practice, being a good lawyer is no longer enough on its own to make a career. There are *a lot* of good practitioners in the industry today. This is why the most valuable lawyers bring something else to the table. They are good lawyers to begin with, but also ones *with clients*. Not only do they bring strong legal skills, but they also bring *revenue*.

THE FREE-AGENT GAME PLAN

So, you are a lawyer. We have covered a lot of ground regarding how law firms work today. What should you be taking away from this?

Above all, you should start to view yourself as a *free agent*.

As noted earlier, most lawyers previously viewed themselves as loyal, lifelong members of the law firm they joined out of law school. Moving away from their firm was somewhat rare. Yet today, with the shift toward merit-based compensation and the stratification of partners within firms, lawyers' careers are different. They need to play a different game.

As firms have largely transformed themselves into meritocracies with multiple classes of lawyers (e.g., equity partner, non-equity partner, Of Counsel, staff attorney, associate), you must understand that your standing within a firm is not guaranteed for any length of time. Some firms reevaluate their partners every single year. Others are more lenient and evaluate their lawyers on a three-year window to account for illness, family deaths, and other personal matters that can affect production. Yet whatever the time frame, your standing within your firm is only as good as your production in the most recent evaluation period.

It does not do you any favors to hold on to a "lifer" mentality. Most lawyers today understand this. Yes, some retain a degree of loyalty to their firms, but nothing like it used to be. In today's market, if a lawyer can improve his financial situation by 20 percent or better, he will probably leave at the first good opportunity to do so. That is market reality in today's legal industry.

Naturally, law firms do not like this view and lament the free-agent mentality. While that is understandable, it should be noted that loyalty is a two-way street. Many law firms are not reluctant to reduce a partner's points and/or compensation when his production suffers. This makes sense. Law firm leaders have businesses to run, some of them very large businesses with revenues in the hundreds of millions of dollars. These leaders cannot retain and sufficiently compensate their best performers if they are spending too much money on those who perform less. The leaders have to do what they believe is best for the firm, even if it displeases certain members.

However, these same leaders should not be surprised when an individual lawyer decides that leaving her firm is in the best interests of her family and her career. The lawyer's lateral move is the other side of the same coin.

Everyone has to do what is in their best interests. That is true whether the party in question is a law firm (and its leaders) or an individual lawyer. *Everyone* is a free agent.

Again, this all makes perfect sense in today's economic landscape. With the advances in technology and the abundance of opportunities, the free-agent mentality has become an essential feature of the gig economy. People today have an unprecedented ability to work as much as they want, how they want, when they want, and where they want.

As the economic engines of the legal industry, lawyers are really no different. They are the revenue generators for law firms and for themselves. It only makes sense that many of them seek opportunities where they can maximize the amount of revenue they generate and thereby maximize their personal income. In today's legal market, it only makes sense for you to view yourself as a free agent too.

WHAT SHOULD THEY TEACH IN LAW SCHOOL?

If the dynamics of law firms have changed, and the relationships between lawyers and their firms have changed, should there be changes in what is taught within America's law schools? After all, law schools are the foundation of the entire legal industry. All of the lawyers in America (with a few unusual exceptions) began their legal careers when they enrolled as first-year law students (1Ls) in one of the nation's more than 200 law schools.

Perhaps better than any other institutions, law schools teach the essential life skills of verbal communication, written communication, persuasion, listening, and critical thinking. These skills are of paramount importance to lawyers and nonlawyers alike. I cannot imagine any educational institution that does a better job of teaching these than a good law school. Although I have not practiced law in over 20 years, I use all of those skills every single day in my business. There is a *lot* that law schools get right.

In addition, I am of course a strong supporter of the essentials that law students learn in the field—including the Constitution in Con Law, the rules in Civil Procedure, and liability in Torts. Certainly, learning the subject matters that comprise the law is an indispensable part of a legal education.

Yet much of the current curriculum, in most law schools, is focused on legal theory as opposed to practical education. This is by design. Most law schools have long maintained that their primary purpose is to teach students how to think, specifically how to "think like a lawyer."

In recent years, more and more law students have pushed back on this idea. Their primary complaint is that they pay a great sum of money and spend three years of their lives attending law school, but when they graduate, they have no idea how to actually be a lawyer. In their view, there is too much theory and not enough practical instruction in their education. In response to this, some law professors and law school administrators counter that law school is not a trade school. Moreover, they continue, law schools have already put more emphasis on clinics, trial advocacy, internships, and other programs for the express purpose of providing more practical instruction in addition to legal theory.

Although I can understand both sides of this issue, and I truly believe a good law school education is invaluable, I believe that the more practical instruction an educational institution can provide, the better. Education has become so expensive that it is reasonable for students to expect to learn more practical skills when they are in school.

With that being said, I believe there is one practical skill that all law schools should teach, and to my knowledge, this skill is not specifically taught in any American law schools: how to sell—or, as it is referred to in the legal industry, "conduct business development."

I realize this idea is appalling to law school professors, and probably to many law school deans as well. However, as someone who has worked in and studied the legal employment market across the country for well over 20 years, I can tell you unequivocally that the ability to bring in business is the single most important skill a lawyer in private practice can have. This assumes, of course, the lawyer is a good attorney. As previously mentioned, being a good lawyer is "table stakes." Someone who is not considered a good lawyer is not even a part of the conversation.

If law schools taught future lawyers how to bring in clients, how to develop business, how to cross-sell different practice areas, and how to provide additional solutions—in other words, how to sell—it would be the most practical and beneficial education its students could receive. This would not be too much of a stretch beyond the standard curriculum. Schools already teach communication skills, critical thinking skills, and listening skills. Sales/business development is a natural extension of what is already being taught.

Furthermore, the bottom line is that everyone is in sales. When students or new lawyers look for jobs, they are selling themselves. Litigators sell their arguments to juries and judges. Transactional lawyers sell their positions to their clients and opposing counsel. In-house lawyers sell their opinions to the companies that employ them. Law school administrators themselves sell their schools to alumni and donors in order to raise funds, and to prospective law students for attendance.

Everyone is in sales, whether they want to be or not. If law schools accepted this fact and included professional sales training as part of the curriculum, it would transform the careers of many of their law students.

Regardless of whether law schools decide to implement sales education as part of their curriculum, there are practical steps that you, as a practicing attorney, can take to improve your skills when it comes to business development (i.e., selling). If you have a mentor or colleague in your firm who is a top rainmaker, ask her for guidance and suggestions. Also, there are countless books, classes, and training programs on sales and rainmaking. Most importantly, it takes a plan and the consistent execution of that plan. Do yourself a huge favor and get started on it today. It is literally the best career move you can make.

Acquiring Legal Talent: Lateral Hiring in Law Firms

CHAPTER 5

WHY FIRMS HIRE LATERALS

IF YOU ARE THE LEADER OF A LAW FIRM, YOU PROBABLY know that, ultimately, law firms can grow in one of two ways: organically or by lateral talent acquisition (including law firm mergers and group hires). By organic growth, I am referring to the process of recruiting law school students, hiring them out of law school, and then training and developing them until they become productive, profitable lawyers.

I want to emphasize that organic growth is very important, and many firms have a robust clerkship program for this very purpose. Even law firms that excel at lateral hiring usually devote some amount of time and resources to organic growth. Why?

There are several reasons firms continue to engage in organic growth efforts. First, hiring graduating law students keeps the firm young. By constantly injecting new blood, law firms decrease the chances of becoming stale and stagnant. Second, firms believe they have better control over their culture if some of their lawyers "grew up" in the firm and never picked up "bad habits" elsewhere. Third, by hiring Summer Clerks and graduating law students, a law firm sends a message to law schools that it is a player and an active, healthy organization. This matters because law schools remain influential to many lawyers throughout their careers.

The problem with organic growth, of course, is that it is a very slow process. When a firm hires a new lawyer, that is often after her clerkship during the summer after her second year of law school. The firm has to wait another year before she graduates and takes the Bar Exam. Then, assuming she does not spend a year or two as a judicial clerk, she will work as an associate, usually for seven to ten years. After that, it typically takes several more years before she has developed true expertise in her practice area or, of equal importance, has become an expert in bringing in clients.

If your firm wants to grow—and that should be nearly all of the time—you do not want to wait ten or more years for every hire to become a truly valuable contributor. In fact, you do not want to wait ten or more months, although sometimes that is unavoidable. You want to grow now. Your firm has opportunities now. Your clients have urgent matters now. Thus, lateral hiring should become a priority, if it was not already.

THE BIG PICTURE

Lateral hiring. It is certainly a big topic in law firms these days. Law firm partners want to know why their firm spends so much time and money on it. It is expensive. It seems to take up *a lot* of firm leadership's time and a big slice of the firm's budget.

If you are a law firm leader, you want to know how to do it better. For most firms, lateral hiring works some of the time, and other times it does not.

First, why do firms engage in lateral hiring? Why is it such a big topic? The main answer is this: **lateral hiring is the best, most effective way for law firms to increase their revenues and profits**. It is *the* main strategy law firms use to grow their businesses. They *need* to do it. Even if some firms want to grow more slowly than others, the old saying is true: in business, you are either growing or you are dying.

Lateral hiring is one of those terms you hear a lot, but not everyone agrees on its meaning. Again, as mentioned at the beginning of this book: *When we refer to laterals throughout this book, we are talking about partner-level lawyers who have moved from one law firm to another, or who are considering such a move. We are not referring to lawyers who move in-house or into government positions, nor are we talking about associate-level attorneys unless otherwise stated.*

Why do we use this special term? What makes this different from other kinds of hiring?

Hiring a lateral attorney is unique because it directly brings in additional revenue to your firm. Therefore, a lateral hire is really quite similar to an acquisition by a corporation. If it is done correctly, the hiring or acquiring party conducts due diligence on cultural fit, as well as the financial aspects of the deal. Questions are asked and discussed at length: Is it accretive? Is it strategic? What primary purpose does it serve? Those are all high-level questions asked when a company is considering an acquisition, and those are the same questions that should be asked in a lateral hiring situation.

Similarly, a lateral hire can be viewed as a type of asset purchase. The hiring law firm is making a significant investment in an asset (i.e., the lateral attorney) with the expectation of receiving a healthy return on that investment. This is analogous to a business purchasing an asset for the purpose of generating a healthy return on investment (ROI).

Now, let's go over in more detail the reasons your firm should conduct lateral hiring.

PURE GROWTH

So you want to grow your firm. While increasing revenues and profits is the primary reason law firms engage in lateral hiring, that does not tell the entire story. There are different types of law firm growth, all of which use lateral hiring as the main instrument through which the growth is achieved.

The first type is *pure growth*, meaning law firms add laterals simply to increase their revenues and add to their attorney roster. In this instance, law firms are not particular about practice areas, provided the laterals' practice areas are compatible with the firm's overall practice. Law firms frequently find themselves wanting to increase their presence in a given market, so they add laterals in any compatible practice area. Stated differently, these firms hire laterals because there is strength in numbers.

In addition to headcount and revenue growth, there are often strategic reasons firms add laterals. These reasons depend on your firm's size, practice focus, geographic footprint, financial performance, and other factors. Some of the more common include the following:

GEOGRAPHIC EXPANSION

Perhaps your firm desires to open an office in a new city. Ideally, this desire is driven directly by client request or by the sound belief that having a physical presence in a given city will result in more business from existing clients or new clients. A direct client request is often the best reason to open an office in a new market. When a good client specifically says, "If you had an office in XYZ city with boots on the ground, I would start sending our work in that market to you," that is a great reason to open an office in XYZ city, assuming, of course, the volume of promised work is sufficient.

Every once in a while, you will hear about a law firm opening an office in another city by having one of their current lawyers physically move there. The lawyer who moves often does so for personal reasons or sometimes for business reasons—to be closer to a key client, for example, or to return to the lawyer's hometown.

A more common way to expand into a new geographic market is with a lateral hire in that market. Sometimes this is a group hire, which is a topic we will cover later in this book. Whether it is with an individual lateral or a group, a lateral hire is usually the most effective way for a law firm to expand into a new city. I would advise you, of course, to be selective and maintain your usual standards to the extent possible when expanding into a new market through a lateral hire.

PRACTICE AREA EXPERTISE

As touched on before, another common reason your firm would hire laterals is to acquire practice area expertise. Depending on the size of your firm and its overall service offerings, hiring a lateral attorney because he or she can bring a genuine expertise to your firm is one of the best reasons to hire a lateral attorney, assuming the lateral fits financially and culturally.

An attorney subject matter expert who has a practice that currently does not exist in the hiring firm, or who can add depth and bench strength to an existing practice, can be tremendously valuable in both the short term and long term. In fact, experts are sometimes hired as laterals even if they do not have a substantial book of business.

Sometimes these attorneys come from the government, from an in-house legal department, or even from an executive position in corporate America. Such attorneys frequently will not bring any portable business with them from Day One, but their backgrounds are such that business is expected to be generated because of their reputations and knowledge.

Even if they never become rainmakers—and many of them do—they can be valuable service partners because of their subject matter expertise.

SUPERSTARS

On a related note, sometimes law firms hire lateral attorneys because they are superstars. A lawyer earns the label of "superstar" by being widely recognized as an accomplished, highly successful attorney with a substantial reputation. These lawyers are coveted as laterals because merely having them as partners in the firm is immensely valuable.

Frequently, these superstars are major rainmakers, but not always. Superstars are hired for their name recognition. The expectation is their reputations will result in business and greater opportunities for the firm that hired them.

Common examples would include former members of Congress, US Attorneys, Attorneys General, Cabinet members, and other high-profile attorneys. These types of well-known individuals can add a level of cachet to your firm, simply by being a part of it. Also, these lawyers usually generate a significant amount of business after they have settled into their new firms.

ACQUISITION OF NEW CLIENTS

One of the great benefits of hiring a lateral, and in fact one of the primary reasons for hiring a lateral, is the acquisition of new clients. All law firms want to acquire new clients, and there are only two ways for a firm to do so.

The first is to market to a potential client, call on that client, work to develop a relationship with that client, and hope that client will start sending some business to your firm and build up from there.

The second is to find a lawyer who has already done all of those things and then hire that lawyer into your firm.

NEW OFFERINGS TO EXISTING CLIENTS

An excellent lateral hire often creates a situation in which your firm can offer new services to your current clients. This can sometimes be because the lateral has unique expertise or has the reputation of being a superstar, as mentioned earlier. Or it can simply be that the lateral is a good lawyer and provides additional strength to your firm. This alone can persuade a client to begin using your firm for matters that were previously sent elsewhere.

PSYCHOLOGICAL EFFECTS

A lateral hire is a big deal. Obviously, it is a big deal for the lateral. It is one of the most significant events in his career. But it is also a big deal for your law firm, your partners, and your clients.

There is a definite psychological impact to making a lateral hire. When your firm announces it is bringing on a lateral attorney, that is a win for your law firm. That is a victory. Presumably, the lateral is a good lawyer with good numbers and is the kind of lawyer many firms would like to have. However, your competitors did not land this lateral. Your firm did.

That is a signal to your firm, and to the partnership, that things are going well. It is validation. "Here is a desirable attorney who probably has options for where to pursue his career, and he chose us."

It also sends a signal to both your current and prospective clients. They should be notified of lateral hires and informed that this is a very positive development for the firm. It reinforces to the client that they made the right decision retaining your firm. This has a positive psychological impact on them too.

Finally, it sends a signal to the legal community. The legal community, including your competitors, notices when a reputable attorney decides to join your law firm. It indicates to them that your firm is a place where winners go to practice law. Moreover, it plants a seed—maybe a tiny seed, but a seed nonetheless—that your firm may be one to consider if they ever decide to explore a lateral move themselves.

CHAPTER 6

WHY LAWYERS MAKE LATERAL MOVES

NOW, LET'S LOOK AT THE OTHER SIDE: WHY LAWYERS make lateral moves.

Although this chapter addresses the individual lawyers (prospective laterals), it also will be instructive to you if you are a law firm leader. It will help improve your firm's lateral hiring, as well as help you understand why lawyers might have made lateral moves away from your firm in the past. So, firm leaders, this chapter is also for you. Prospective laterals, this may help guide you through the thought process behind a very important career step.

Not surprisingly, the main reason you might want to make a lateral move is to increase your personal compensation. But there are many nuances around how your compensation will be affected by such a move, as well as other benefits to consider. Let's look at more specifics, knowing that ultimately they all have an impact on your personal income.

FIRM COMPENSATION SYSTEMS

This is a big one on several different levels. First, certain compensation systems are more attractive to certain lawyers. Some lawyers do better when more credit is given for business development and originations. Some lawyers do better when more credit is given for personal production/working attorney revenues. Some lawyers prefer that seniority and longevity with the firm be given more weight; other lawyers do not want seniority to be a factor at all.

The bottom line with compensation systems is this: if a new firm can show you that they would increase your compensation by 20 percent or more based on the same numbers you have with your current firm, simply because of how those numbers are calculated and credited, then that is an excellent reason to seriously consider a lateral move.

In addition to how the numbers are calculated, a better overall process for determining attorney compensation can be a reason you might want to make a lateral move. Does your firm have an open and transparent compensation plan, or is it more of the "smoke-filled back room"? Is there a compensation committee whose members are elected, or is there an oligarchy or a benevolent dictator who makes compensation decisions? Is it purely formulaic, with no gray areas, or is it more subjective? If you are not pleased with your compensation, do you have the ability to seek redress?

All types of compensation systems have their pros and cons. Each of the various systems will appeal to certain lawyers and not appeal to others.

Nonetheless, it should be noted that I hear far fewer complaints about transparent systems. I have seen attorneys who were making very good money—probably better than they should have been making, based on their numbers—make lateral moves for the same amount of money simply because the new firm had an open compensation system. The lawyers would *know* they were being compensated fairly, and that was enough for them to make a lateral move.

Even if they were being compensated fairly at the old firm, and they often were, they could not get past the fact that they did not know with certainty whether they were being treated well compared to other lawyers at the firm. So they left. As a lawyer, a more transparent system might be very compelling to you.

BILLING RATE ISSUES

Another common reason you might seek a lateral move is because of bill rates. If you are a lawyer who practices in a large firm, particularly in one that is national or international, perhaps you experience rate pressure from your firm's management. The firm wants you to increase your rates so that you are billing X and above on all of your matters.

Guess who does not want to pay X per hour? Your clients. Your clients like you and your work. However, they are watching expenses like a hawk, and it seems like they just agreed to a raise in rates a few months ago. It was actually a couple of years ago, but they could swear it was more recent than that. Plus, these clients know there are *a lot* of good lawyers out there, and surely some of them would be more reasonable about billing rates.

So, as the lawyer, you are caught in the middle. The firm wants you to raise rates, but you fear losing clients if you even think about raising rates. *And* you are certain you can increase your book of business considerably if you can lower your rates just a little bit. You know there is new business you can land, and current clients you can get more work from, if you only had a little bit of rate flexibility.

But your firm management says no because if they bend the rate structure for you, then they have to do it for everyone. So what do you do? Oftentimes, you look for a firm that offers more rate flexibility or even outright autonomy. You look for a firm that would love to have your practice and clients at 80 percent of X because their overhead is lower or their model is different. That is when you might make a lateral move.

The other side of billing rates can also be a good reason. Sometimes, lawyers find themselves in a firm that cannot fully utilize their practice and expertise. These lawyers are somewhat stuck at a certain bill rate because of their firm, but they know at a different firm—maybe a bigger firm with more attorneys, a larger geographic footprint, and more practice area offerings, or a firm that is simply perceived to be a better firm—they could increase their rates easily with little resistance from their clients. Increased rates, of course, lead to more revenue, which leads to higher compensation. If you are in this situation, you might want to make a lateral move as well.

CLIENT CONFLICTS

Occasionally, a lawyer will find herself in a position to land a great client, one that will generate significant business, sometimes even across multiple practice areas in different cities. However, that lawyer is prevented from taking on that new client because that new client would create a major conflict with an existing, valuable client of the firm.

A classic, simplified example would be if you had a close relationship with the General Counsel of FedEx. He tells you that you can have a lot of FedEx legal work, but your current firm represents UPS, and they will not let you take on FedEx as a client.

In a situation like this, you would usually make the lateral move. These conflict situations are often beyond the former firm's control.

MANAGEMENT AND LEADERSHIP

As with any employer, management and leadership of a law firm have a large impact on job satisfaction. You might make a lateral move away from your current firm if you do not like how the firm is being run.

Perhaps the chemistry between you and a key leader is just not good. Or maybe you dislike the management style. Some firms encourage independence and autonomy while others are more rigid. Sometimes lawyers feel excluded from having any input or influence in the firm, and that frustrates them.

Further, you could have concerns over the future of the firm. Do you have confidence in the firm leadership and its strategic plans? Does the firm leadership have a growth strategy? Is there a vision for the future?

No one wants to be on a sinking ship. No one wants to be in a firm that has no direction and no vision. More and more, lawyers today pay close attention not only to how the firm is doing in the present, but also to what the future is likely to hold for the firm.

A quick note to the law firm leaders: is the firm adding or losing laterals? This is a big one. Almost all firms will lose attorneys, but overall, is the firm adding more than it is losing, or vice versa? In Chapter 5, we noted the psychological benefits to your firm if you are adding good laterals. Well, the inverse of that is also certainly true.

If your firm is losing more lawyers than it is adding, not only will revenues decrease (and probably firm profits, assuming the departing lawyers were productive), but there is also a real psychological loss that comes with losing headcount. Your firm's lawyers will start looking around and asking themselves, "Well, if he left, and she left, and they left, and they are all good, productive lawyers, maybe I should think about leaving too." No one wants to be the last person standing.

FINANCIAL PERFORMANCE

Of course, you want to be at a firm with great financial performance. This is your bottom line. Law firms that have lower profits per partner, lower revenues per lawyer, capital calls, rising overhead, personal guarantees, and/or excessive debt are most likely going to experience lateral departures—for good reason.

Unfortunately, the departure of profitable lawyers exacerbates a firm's financial struggles. This will not matter if you are a departing lateral, but if you are a leader, you can end up with a vicious cycle, and sometimes even a death spiral for the firm.

MARKETING AND BUSINESS DEVELOPMENT

Let's say, as a lawyer, your current firm is still not especially interested in having an active, aggressive, professional business development strategy. Despite the importance of marketing and business development to a successful law firm and a healthy practice, some firms have legacy, institutional clients that they assume will always be with them. Others are simply happy with what they have and do not want to make the investment in time and resources to increase their client base.

If you are a good lawyer, and especially if you are a rainmaker, you have options. These firms are highly vulnerable to losing someone like you.

Rainmakers are, as we have already established and as the market has determined, the most valuable lawyers in a firm, especially during tough times. As such, you need—and deserve—support. You need marketing assistance. You need help cross-selling across practice areas and offices. You need the firm to support your efforts at speaking and publishing and attending conferences. All these things help the true rainmaker bring in more business. If your current firm is not supportive of these activities, then you might consider looking elsewhere because there are plenty of firms out there that would love to take on the best rainmakers, invest in both time and resources, and watch your practice increase to the benefit of both you and the new firm.

Law firm leaders, watch out for this situation, and make sure you are supporting your rainmakers well.

MANDATORY RETIREMENT

Mandatory retirement policies have become an increasingly common reason for lawyers to explore lateral moves. As baby boomers have reached retirement age, many of them have realized they do not want to retire—or, in some cases, cannot afford to retire. Moreover, they are often in good shape mentally and physically, enjoy practicing law, have strong relationships with their clients, and, of course, enjoy earning a high income.

This book is not intended to discuss generational conflicts and whether the older generation is hanging on too long, or whether the younger generation is being impatient. What I will say is that through the years, law firms have lost a significant number of productive, talented attorneys because of their firm's mandatory retirement policies. Lawyers who reached 65, or even 60 in some cases, were forced to transition their clients, lose their equity, accept lower income, or even leave their old firms entirely.

For some lawyers, this was fine. For others, this was not acceptable. So what did they do? They took their practices, their clients, their production, and their profitability to other firms that embraced them. These new firms wanted these lawyers and their clients, and the situations usually resulted in a win-win arrangement.

People live longer than they used to and are also in good health much longer. It is not at all uncommon for lawyers to remain highly productive well into their 70s. Only a few decades ago, that would have been highly unusual.

I certainly understand the reasons for mandatory retirement policies, and I am not arguing for or against them. However, firms that maintain more traditional types of mandatory retirement policies are vulnerable to losing a lot of great legal talent, and clients, to firms that have less traditional retirement policies.

Even if you are a young lawyer, this is certainly an important consideration to have for your future.

PRACTICING ON AN ISLAND

It is not uncommon, as a lawyer, to feel socially isolated at your current firm. This is particularly true if you are practicing in a highly specialized area with few colleagues, or if you are in a smaller office of a large firm or one that is geographically isolated. Although lawyers often work individually on specific tasks, most attorneys in law firms like to be part of a team. They like to have colleagues with whom they can collaborate and brainstorm. They like to have service partners and associates to handle certain tasks, which frees them up to handle other responsibilities. They like having other lawyers around them, particularly other lawyers with expertise in complementary practice areas.

They also like to have resources and the support of law firm leadership. Many firms tend to focus their resources on certain offices or practice areas. If you have a good practice, but it is not in one of the favored markets or practice areas, maybe you feel neglected or like you are not one of the "chosen ones." This is when you might consider looking at other firms.

AUTONOMY

Autonomy is an important issue for most lawyers. It certainly matters when it comes to billing rates, as we touched on earlier. At some law firms, firm management tells the lawyers what their bill rate will be and that is it. At other firms, there is a rate sheet or a range within which the lawyers can bill.

Some firms offer their lawyers total autonomy in their bill rates. These firms typically give their attorneys revenue goals, not hourly goals. They say to their lawyers, "You can bill $1,000 per hour or $100 per hour. We do not care. But your revenue goal is X. How many hours it takes you to get there is up to you." Certainly, there are good reasons for firms to control or manage their lawyers' billing rates. But as it pertains to lateral movement, most lawyers, understandably, prefer as much autonomy over their billing rates as possible.

Of course, autonomy extends beyond billing rates. Having input on major firm decisions and having a high level of control over how you practice, market, and develop clients are all important factors when assessing satisfaction with your current law firm.

In fact, although it is rare for lawyers to make a lateral move that requires a reduction in their compensation, I have seen lawyers do just that in order to gain more autonomy over their law practice.

Firm leaders: do not underestimate the importance of autonomy. It matters—to a few lawyers, even more than money.

DIVERSITY

As we all know, diversity is a very important issue in the legal community. One of the main reasons diversity is so important to law firms, aside from the inherent value in different perspectives, is because it is important to the rest of corporate America. When clients tell their law firms they want to see a diverse group of lawyers on their matters, then it becomes even more important.

Firm leaders, if your firm has not had much success increasing its diversity, and you have lawyers whose clients have told them they expect a diverse group of lawyers to be working on their matters, then you need to realize those lawyers may be considering a lateral move. Those lawyers do not want to lose their clients, obviously. If moving to a firm with greater diversity increases their odds of successfully retaining those clients, then they will make a lateral move to keep them.

PLATFORM AND FOOTPRINT

The most likely reason you would make a lateral move as a lawyer would be to join a firm with a larger geographic footprint and a more robust platform for your practice. This is all about retaining and increasing your representation of existing clients and developing new clients.

Most people, regardless of their situation, want to move up. They want to do more. They want to get bigger. If you are practicing in a firm with a single office, then a move to a regional firm with five offices is appealing. You can represent your clients with boots on the ground in five cities, as opposed to just one. If that regional firm offers practice areas that your current firm does not have, then all of a sudden, you can cross-sell your clients on matters you never could before. Your old firm did not have an intellectual property (IP) practice. Your new firm has ten IP lawyers, and your client has IP needs. It does not take long to connect those dots.

If you, as a lawyer, are practicing in a regional firm, and you are approached about joining a national firm with offices across the country (and even beyond) and even more practice area expertise, then the same principle applies. Plus, in a larger firm with more bench strength, you now have the chance to go after certain clients, and certain types of business, that you never could before. Some clients and some matters are simply not available for firms below a certain size. Now, you can go after new business, and it is probably business that pays you higher rates than you have been getting. You are moving up in your practice.

I am not saying bigger is always better. I am simply saying this is probably the most common reason lawyers make lateral moves.

Law firm leaders: you should realize your lawyers are constantly being recruited by firms with larger footprints and more resources. While you cannot control this, you can control how you defend against it. First, pay your lawyers as well as you can. Second, emphasize the advantages your firm offers. For example, smaller firms can often provide their partners with more autonomy and input into firm decisions. Also, smaller firms frequently have a greater sense of camaraderie than larger firms. Whatever advantages your firm possesses, emphasize them as part of your retention strategy.

CHAPTER 7

TIPS FOR SUCCESSFUL LATERAL HIRING

AS A FIRM LEADER, YOU KNOW THAT YOUR FIRM IS PROBably engaged in some amount of lateral hiring or is at least seriously considering it. Although it is certainly not a perfect strategy, the fact remains that lateral hiring is the most effective way for law firms to grow. There really are not any alternatives other than group hires and law firm mergers. Having placed a number of practice groups with law firms and facilitated more than a few successful law firm mergers, I can tell you that both of those are really just different types of lateral hiring, albeit with more complexity and certain different issues.

So, if your firm is going to be in the business of lateral hiring, let's talk about some ways in which your firm can improve its lateral hiring efforts. Let's begin with an overview, which can be called the three Cs.

THE THREE CS

With all of the strategies, tactics, tips, and suggestions through-out this book to help you with lateral talent acquisition, I can offer you a quick snapshot summarizing this information. Basically, you need to attract prospective lateral hires with the three Cs: cash, culture, and camaraderie.

First, let's talk cash, or compensation.

There is no question that the ultimate driver for most lateral moves is money. Most lawyers consider and make these moves because they believe the financial opportunity at New Firm is better than the financial opportunity at Old Firm. If a lateral does not believe she will make more money at New Firm, then most of the time she is not going to make that lateral move. Even if the projected increase in compensation is more long term than short, oftentimes that is enough incentive to make the lateral move.

Note that when I say "cash," I am not talking solely about buying lawyers, although that does happen sometimes. Cash, in this instance, refers to the lawyer's ability to make more money on an ongoing basis by making a lateral move from Old Firm to New Firm. Sometimes, this ability to make more money is because of the compensation structure at New Firm. Sometimes, it is because of ongoing client conflicts at Old Firm that will not be present at New Firm, thereby greatly increasing the lateral's originations. Sometimes, the expected increase in compensation is because of New Firm's greater footprint, or deeper bench, or broader practice area expertise.

The specifics will vary depending on Old Firm, New Firm, and the lateral in question. The bottom line, however, remains the same. If your law firm wants to grow by adding lateral talent, you need to provide a clear avenue through which a lateral can make more money there than she can with her current law firm.

Next, a potential lateral hire is going to be looking for the right culture.

This is the second most important factor when laterals consider moving to a new law firm. But what is culture, anyway? It is one of those words that is used frequently, probably too frequently, but it is important because culture really matters to most laterals. For our purposes, culture is defined as the behaviors and customs within an organization. In other words, culture is "how we do things around here."

A law firm's policies, procedures, values, ethical standards, attitudes, goals, and conduct all comprise the firm's culture. And it is true that each firm has a unique culture. The firm's culture is displayed in its compensation system, its work ethic, its dress code, how the lawyers practice law, how the lawyers treat each other, how the lawyers treat nonlawyer staff, the energy of the firm, and the overall feeling or vibe of the firm.

If you want to attract the right lateral talent, your firm needs to maintain an attractive culture. Very few laterals are attracted to negativity, selfishness, rudeness, or secrecy. The law firms with the best cultures actively promote courtesy, positivity, teamwork, and transparency.

I have seen a number of prospective laterals decide not to join a law firm just because of its culture, even when the laterals would have increased their compensation by making the lateral move. Although culture does not carry the same weight as compensation when laterals are deciding whether to change firms, it is nonetheless an important factor to get right.

Last, for many lawyers, the sense of camaraderie within a law firm can make or break the decision to change law firms.

In fact, in some cases, the sense of camaraderie at a lawyer's current firm will prevent her from changing to another, even if that would make the most financial sense. Like all organizations, law firms are made of human beings and human relationships. Professional friendships develop, and some lawyers, even in today's age of free agency, feel a sense of loyalty to their current partners and friends within their firms.

For New Firm—the firm that is actively recruiting laterals—a recommended practice is to display a sense of friendship and camaraderie, assuming, of course, it is genuine. If your existing lawyers have this sense of friendship and camaraderie, get them involved in your firm's lateral recruiting process. Let prospective laterals see the strong personal and professional relationships that exist within your firm. Again, cash is king, and money will always be the largest drive for most laterals, but relationships and a strong sense of camaraderie can be very persuasive.

> The three Cs are a general summary. For those seeking a more detailed look at how firms can improve their lateral hiring success, here are a number of suggestions.

PAY PREMIUMS FOR SUPERSTARS

First, to land the highest-quality legal talent, you have to pay for it. You have to give laterals a reason to leave their current firm, which at worst has for them the comfort of familiarity. You are asking them to move to what is largely an unknown entity.

Absent something unusual, at a minimum, the best legal talent will be looking for a way to increase their pay. Sometimes this can come in the form of performance bonuses, but sometimes these top-shelf lawyers will want the increase in the form of their salary. In other words, some will want it guaranteed.

Now, your firm should be *very* cautious when it comes to guaranteed salaries and payments to laterals. The practice of paying exorbitant guaranteed salaries to laterals has brought down a number of firms in past years. Overpayment can also breed heavy resentment among your current partners, in the absence of compelling reasons for the overpayment.

However, in certain situations, and for certain lawyers, paying a premium—that is, paying over and above their current compensation, and over and above what their compensation would normally be at your firm—can make sense. Sometimes, it is the only way you can land a particular lawyer. She is simply not coming otherwise. If you have made an objective analysis of what adding her to the firm would likely mean, and the projected revenues and firm profits are likely to outweigh the expenses by enough margin, then it may be worth the risk.

HIRE IN GROUPS OR ACQUIRE FIRMS

We will cover this in more detail in Chapter 15, but here's a brief overview.

Some law firms have begun to place an emphasis on lateral hiring of groups of lawyers, as opposed to ones and twos. Although hiring a group is a more complex, more expensive transaction, a group can have a much greater and faster impact than hiring an individual lawyer can. Together, they can "move the needle" in a way that almost no individual lawyer can.

A group of laterals, first of all, will generate more revenue than a single lateral. Also, a group is more likely to bring key clients because when an entire group comes, there are fewer remaining lawyers at the old firm who can fight to retain the business. Also, integration into the new firm is usually much easier with a group. Ease of integration is *very* important with all lateral hires.

You could also acquire smaller firms. In this case, the benefits are even more apparent. When the acquired group is an entire firm, there is usually minimal concern about losing clients, and the transition of receivables and collections is much easier.

The major drawbacks to a group hire or firm acquisition are the ones mentioned earlier. It is much more expensive, and requires more capital outlay, than a single hire. It is a more complex transaction because it is a larger group of people. Sometimes, there are cultural conflicts. But if the acquiring firm did its due diligence, these should have been discovered early on in the merger process. Certainly, any potential client conflicts should have been addressed early on in the process as well.

Depending on your firm's needs and your specific reasons for pursuing lateral hires, a group hire or firm merger may make a lot of sense. If you can find the right group or firm as far as practice and economics, have done your due diligence on the cultural fit, and are comfortable with the level of risk involved, then the greater impact of a group hire or firm acquisition can be the ideal growth strategy.

INVOLVE LEADERSHIP IN LATERAL HIRING

Leadership may be the most important component of any law firm's lateral hiring plan. If your firm has a leader who is committed to lateral hiring, and who gets actively involved in speaking to potential laterals and selling your firm to them, then your odds of success in lateral hiring go up significantly.

High-level laterals want to speak to the leadership of the firm, ideally the firm Managing Partner and/or Chair of the Hiring Committee, or the local office Managing Partner. If firm leadership makes lateral hiring a priority, then they will commit the resources to making sure it happens as successfully as possible. This involvement by firm leadership can make all of the difference.

DESIGNATE SOMEONE TO MANAGE THE LATERAL HIRING PROCESS

It is so important to be organized when recruiting lateral attorneys. Most firms with active lateral recruiting programs have one person (or one team in larger firms) who is in charge of the process. This person makes sure nothing falls through the cracks, which can easily happen when you are working with busy lawyers. She is ultimately accountable for making sure the steps in the process are followed, and she holds the others accountable who are responsible for the different steps.

She should have a checklist for each potential lateral under consideration and make sure the right steps are being followed every time. These steps include scheduling interviews, ensuring meetings with practice group heads and firm leadership, conflicts checks, due diligence, answering prospective laterals' questions, conversations with the legal recruiter involved, and completion of the Lateral Partner Questionnaire.

There are numerous steps in the lateral hiring process, and all of them are important. It is essential that firms have a system in place to make sure the correct steps are followed and completed. Thus, it is a good idea to designate someone to keep track of all of this.

ADMINISTER THOROUGH, BUT CONCISE, LPQS

The Lateral Partner Questionnaire (LPQ) is a vital document that your firm must have if it is engaged in lateral hiring. The purpose of the LPQ is to get the most important information about the lateral down on paper. This includes financial data, of course, but the LPQ also asks for details about clients, practice matters, conflicts, employment history, professional history issues such as malpractice claims or lawsuits, and personal history such as crimes or bankruptcies.

When you administer LPQs, make sure they are as thorough as possible so that you inquire about everything you need to cover. However, they do not need to be 30 pages long. Lawyers absolutely *hate* to fill out LPQs. They understand the need for them and will fill them out, but they certainly don't enjoy it. The longer they are, the harder it is to get them completed.

KEEP IT SPEEDY

When it comes to success in lateral hiring, speed is absolutely essential. There is an old saying that time kills all deals. That is certainly the case with most lateral hires. To be sure, some recruiting efforts are drawn out and can go on for months—even two to three years, in rare cases. The longest lateral deal I ever worked on that ended successfully took three years from start to finish. But that is a rare exception. In most cases, it is essential to be decisive, move quickly, and keep the process going.

This is an emotional decision for the lateral, in addition to being a business decision. There are personal relationships at the current firm, the comfort of familiarity, and the constant pull of inertia. In order to overcome these factors, speed is vital. These lateral deals start to create momentum. When momentum is on your side, you have to act if you want to have success.

I am not saying that you should shortcut your process at all. You have to go through your lateral hiring checklist (see earlier in this chapter), and you have to do your due diligence.

However, each step in the process should be done as quickly as possible, and the lateral candidate should be kept apprised on a regular basis regarding what the status is, the progress that is being made, and the estimated time frame for next steps.

The key to speed is not that the hire must be made quickly, but rather that the steps of the hiring process should be performed in a steady, timely manner. Otherwise, it gets pushed to the back burner, no one follows up on the process, and the next thing you know, six months have passed and the lateral is no longer available.

In other words, speed is vital.

TELL SUCCESS STORIES TO YOUR LATERAL CANDIDATES

Here is the last tip for successful lateral hiring: tell candidates about lateral hires at your firm who have been successful. Ideally, have the lateral candidate meet (in person or by video conference) with one or more of your lawyers who are lateral success stories. It is so powerful when one of your lawyers can look a lateral candidate in the eye and tell her, "Moving to this law firm was a great decision for me. The people are very nice, and I increased my book of business by 40 percent within two years. My compensation this year will be higher than it ever was at my old firm."

Stories like that resonate. They are real, and they can be incredibly effective in helping your firm lure the talent you want to add.

THE UNFORTUNATE STATISTICS ON LATERAL HIRING SUCCESS

Lateral hiring is *the* main strategy law firms use to grow their businesses. This is because **lateral hiring is the best, most effective way for law firms to increase their revenues and profits.** The other options are organic growth, which is *very* slow, or group acquisitions and law firm mergers, which, as mentioned earlier, are really just other forms of lateral hiring.

So lateral hiring sounds pretty good. You hire a good lawyer. She brings her clients with her. Law firm revenues and profits increase. Everybody is happy. Right?

Well, I would be remiss not to end this chapter with a brief caveat. Statistically, approximately half of lateral hires are not successful. "Not successful" means either the lateral is gone from the firm that hired her within five years, or she is still at the firm but has not delivered the business she was hired to bring and is just sort of plodding along. Both of these scenarios—the lateral who is gone within five years and the lateral who is plodding along but has underperformed—are money losers for your law firm.

Laterals are expensive. The cost can easily run into the hundreds of thousands of dollars or more. You have to provide compensation and benefits the entire time the lateral is at your firm. You have downtime or lag time when you are paying the lateral before she has collected anything for her work done or brought in the door. You have search firm fees. You have lost time spent on the lateral by your management and other attorneys. All of this adds up to a very expensive endeavor.

This is not to deter you. Ultimately, lateral hiring is really an investment, and it should be viewed as such. Like all investments, a lateral hire can deliver positive returns that make you money, or it can deliver negative returns that cost you money.

If you do it right, and follow the suggestions in this book, then hopefully your firm's investments will result in the addition of talented, profitable attorneys who drive growth to your firm.

SECTION

III

Ethical Considerations in Lateral Hiring

CHAPTER 8

THE FOUR KEY ETHICAL PRINCIPLES

IF YOU ARE GETTING READY TO HIRE A LATERAL OR ONE is leaving your firm, there are ethical issues that you must consider. Of course, some lateral hires are easier than others as far as the ethics are concerned, but certain ethical rules apply to *every* lateral hiring situation. Here is a concise guide.

There are four main ethical principles in a lateral hiring situation:

1. The client's right to choice of counsel
2. The lawyer's right to change firms without restriction
3. Fiduciary obligations owed to the firm and its partners
4. Fiduciary obligations owed to clients

Some of these ethical principles are stated clearly by the Rules of Professional Conduct, and some will be covered by other legal obligations. The ABA Standing Committee on Ethics and Professional Responsibility has said, "The departing lawyer also must consider legal obligations other than ethics rules that apply to [his/her] conduct when changing firms, as well as...fiduciary duties owed [to] the former firm. The law of agency, partnership, property, contracts, and unfair competition impose obligations that are not addressed directly by the Model Rules." (ABA Formal Ethics Opinion 99-414). In other words, the lateral (or "departing lawyer") must be mindful of a number of obligations she has, including but not limited to the ethics rules. We will cover the most important obligations in this chapter.

Because each state has its own Rules of Professional Conduct and other applicable laws, for convenience we will rely on the ABA Model Rules of Professional Conduct and generally accepted statutory provisions. Consulting state-specific cases, statutes, and ethical rules, however, is necessary to ensure compliance in each specific jurisdiction. An attorney's partnership agreement also should be reviewed when an attorney is considering a lateral move.

FOUR ETHICAL PRINCIPLES IN LATERAL HIRING

Let's go over the four main ethical principles in detail.

The first major ethical principle at issue in a lateral hiring situation is the client's right to choice of counsel.

This first ethical principle is established by ABA Model Rules of Professional Conduct, Rule 1.16, Declining or Terminating Representation:

(a) Except as stated in paragraph (c), a lawyer shall not represent a client or, where representation has commenced, shall withdraw from the representation of a client, if…

(3) The lawyer is discharged.

COMMENT (4): A client has a right to discharge a lawyer at any time, with or without cause, subject to liability for payment for the lawyer's services.

This can be considered the most important ethical principle when it comes to lateral hiring. In fact, if not for this principle, there would be no lateral hiring.

The bottom line is this: the client has the right to choose any lawyer he wants to represent him. Period. The law firm does not get to decide. The departing lateral does not get to decide. The client does.

Certainly, there are no ethical issues with working hard to *keep* a client. This applies to both the lateral as well as the former law firm the lateral just left. In fact, this is pretty common. Clients are valuable, obviously, and lawyers and firms are wise to work on keeping them. But the principle remains.

Sometimes lawyers and firms forget this principle, or at least they choose to ignore it. I have worked with laterals in the past who have said to me, "I do not think I can take XYZ client with me if I change firms. My current firm will not let me." Similarly, when attorneys have left law firms, I have heard the law firms say, "We will not let him take ABC company. That client is ours."

In both of these scenarios, the lateral and the law firm are wrong. They do not own the client. The client, and only the client, gets to decide who is going to be his attorney.

The second major ethical principle at issue in a lateral hiring situation is the lawyer's right to change firms.

ABA Model Rules of Professional Conduct, Rule 5.6, Restrictions on Rights to Practice

A lawyer shall not participate in offering or making:

(a) a partnership, shareholders, operating, employment, or other similar type of agreement that restricts the right of a lawyer to practice after termination of the relationship, except an agreement concerning benefits upon retirement; or

(b) an agreement in which a restriction on the lawyer's right to practice is part of the settlement of a client controversy.

Comment:

[1] An agreement restricting the right of lawyers to practice after leaving a firm not only limits their professional autonomy but also limits the freedom of clients to choose a lawyer. Paragraph (a) prohibits such agreements except for restrictions incident to provisions concerning retirement benefits for service with the firm.

It has long been held and upheld that lawyers have the right to change firms at their discretion, and restrictions against this right are invalid. It is for this reason that attorneys do not have noncompete agreements except under certain limited circumstances that do not apply here, as indicated in the comment above.

This ethical principle is tied directly to the first. If the client likes his lawyer but does not like his lawyer's current firm for whatever reason, then the client's choice of counsel is infringed upon if his lawyer cannot change firms. The lawyer's ability to change firms at her discretion is therefore considered an integral part of the client's right to choose the counsel he wants.

The third major ethical principle at issue in a lateral hiring situation is fiduciary obligations to partners.

The third major ethical principle at issue in a lateral hiring situation is not derived from the Rules of Professional Responsibility. Instead, it is the fiduciary duties lawyers owe to their partners. This ethical principle is governed by the Revised Uniform Partnership Act (RUPA).

Note: As is the case throughout this book, and as stated in the Author's Notes, we are using the term "partner" broadly for these purposes. Because every state has its own statutory code with certain variations, we are using the Revised Uniform Partnership Act as our authority for this principle. Most states have adopted RUPA or its forerunner, the Uniform Partnership Act. Also, RUPA applies to limited liability partnerships as well as general partnerships, and most states' limited liability company statutes follow RUPA's organization and logic.

There are two specific sections of RUPA that govern lateral moves for partners:

Section 404. General Standards of Partner's Conduct

(a) The only fiduciary duties a partner owes to the partnership and the other partners are the duty of loyalty and the duty of care set forth in subsections (b) and (c).

(b) A partner's duty of loyalty to the partnership and the other partners is limited to the following:

(1) to account to the partnership and hold as trustee for it any property, profit, or benefit derived by the partner in the conduct and winding up of the partnership business or derived from a use by the partner of partnership property, including the appropriation of a partnership opportunity;

(2) to refrain from dealing with the partnership in the conduct or winding up of the partnership business as or on behalf of a party having an interest adverse to the partnership; and

(3) to refrain from competing with the partnership in the conduct of the partnership business before the dissolution of the partnership.

(c) A partner's duty of care to the partnership and the other partners in the conduct and winding up of the partnership business is limited to refraining from engaging in grossly negligent or reckless conduct, intentional misconduct, or a knowing violation of law.

(d) A partner shall discharge the duties to the partnership and the other partners under this [Act] or under the partnership agreement and exercise any rights consistently with the obligation of good faith and fair dealing.

(e) A partner does not violate a duty or obligation under this [Act] or under the partnership agreement merely because the partner's conduct furthers the partner's own interest.

(f) A partner may lend money to and transact other business with the partnership, and as to each loan or transaction the rights and obligations of the partner are the same as those of a person who is not a partner, subject to other applicable law.

(g) This section applies to a person winding up the partnership business as the personal or legal representative of the last surviving partner as if the person were a partner.

Section 603. Effect of Partner's Dissociation

(b) Upon a partner's dissociation:

(1) the partner's right to participate in the management and conduct of the partnership business terminates, except as otherwise provided in Section 803;

(2) the partner's duty of loyalty under Section 404(b)(3) terminates; and

(3) the partner's duty of loyalty under Section 404(b)(1) and (2) and duty of care under Section 404(c) continue only with regard to matters arising and events occurring before the partner's dissociation, unless the partner participates in winding up the partnership's business pursuant to Section 803.6.

Here is where it gets interesting. This is the ethical principle that arguably is in conflict with the first two.

The first two are pretty straightforward. The client has the right to choose any lawyer he wants. The lawyer has the right to practice at any place she wants. That seems pretty clear.

However, there is a catch. The lawyer, especially if she is a partner, has a *fiduciary* obligation to her firm. Stated differently, the lawyer has an obligation to act in the firm's best interests.

Basically, these fiduciary obligations include the duty to not compete against the current firm and to not use the current firm's assets for personal benefit. Going deeper, these duties require the lateral attorney to:

- not appropriate a partnership opportunity
- not compete against the firm within the scope of the firm's business
- not engage in willful or intentional misconduct

Looking at these obligations the lateral attorney owes to her partners, it becomes more complicated. When you consider what she is *not* allowed to do, you can see that a lateral must be very careful in how she makes a lateral move so that she does not violate her fiduciary duties.

Later in this book, we will look closely at some do's and don'ts, *but a general rule of thumb is that a lawyer may* prepare *to compete while still at her old firm but may not* actually *compete.*

The fourth major ethical principle at issue in a lateral hiring situation is fiduciary duties to clients.

If you are a lawyer, the fiduciary duties you owe to your clients is arguably the most important principle in our entire legal system.

The fiduciary duty an attorney owes to her clients during a lateral move can be defined in a number of ways, but a simple definition is this: **an attorney must act in the client's best interests, not the attorney's**.

ABA Model Rules of Professional Conduct, Rule 1.4, Communications

(b) A lawyer shall explain a matter to the extent reasonably necessary to permit the client to make informed decisions regarding the representation.

With regard to a lateral departure, ABA Formal Ethics Opinion 99-414 provides great insight on this duty and the ethical principle at issue:

> A lawyer's ethical obligations upon withdrawal from one firm to join another derive from the concepts that clients' interests must be protected and that each client has the right to choose the departing lawyer or the firm, or another lawyer to represent him. The departing lawyer and the responsible members of her firm who remain must take reasonable measures to assure that the withdrawal is accomplished without material adverse effect on the interests of clients with active matters upon which the lawyer currently is working. The departing lawyer and responsible members of the law firm who remain have an ethical obligation to assure that prompt notice is given to clients on whose active matters she currently is working.

When it comes to lateral hiring, acting in the client's best interests means the lateral attorney must communicate regularly with the client and must disclose material information in a timely manner. Clearly, material information includes the fact that an attorney with whom a client has had significant personal contact is leaving that firm. The client needs to be notified in a timely manner.

But exactly what does that mean? What does timely mean? When should the departing lawyer notify the client? When should she notify her firm? How can she make sure she handles those notifications so that she does not violate the ethical duties she owes to both the client and her former firm?

Before answering those questions, let's summarize the ethical principles and inherent tension between them in many lateral hiring situations:

- The lateral has the right to change firms.
- She cannot solicit clients away from her current firm because of her fiduciary obligations to her current firm and partners.
- The lateral also owes a fiduciary obligation to her client to keep the client informed of all material information.
- A client's counsel's changing firms is clearly material information.

So how does the lateral, and her new law firm, handle this situation in a manner that does not violate any ethical rules?

Ultimately, this comes down to the right notification and timing.

CHAPTER 9

NOTIFICATION AND TIMING OF A LATERAL'S DEPARTURE

FIRST, LET'S LOOK AT THE IDEAL SITUATION. IDEALLY, IF you are a departing lateral, you give notice to your old firm that you are leaving before you notify any of your clients. This is what the Model Rules require. Then both you and your former firm determine which clients are "your current clients." You both send joint letters to all of the clients with whom you worked closely or with whom you had significant personal contact (i.e., "your current clients"). This is also required by the Model Rules (see ABA Formal Ethics Opinion 99-414, at 4).

This joint notification approach is clearly favored by the courts and the ABA Formal Ethics Opinions. If both sides agree, then joint letters should be sent to the client regarding your intended departure. The point of the letter is to notify the client that their lawyer is moving to a new firm. Then the client can do one of three things regarding their existing legal matters:

1. Continue to use the legal services of the current firm
2. Transfer the legal matter(s) to the departing lawyer and her new firm
3. Engage another (third) lawyer or law firm to represent them

This letter must clearly state that the client has the sole right to decide who will continue or complete the representation.

Furthermore, the letter should state the timing of the departure, the departing lawyer's new association (i.e., the new firm), and the willingness of both the old firm and new firm to continue the current representation of the client.

The letter should also seek client direction regarding the transfer of files. As it is a joint letter, as a practical matter, it will not contain disparaging comments about either party, nor will the letter urge the client to continue with one relationship or another. Nevertheless, the opinions expressly proscribe both. If the firm and the departing lawyer cannot agree on the language of a letter, then separate letters can be sent and those should also not contain any disparaging language.

Email is perfectly fine for these notification letters. In fact, it is preferable to regular mail because clients need to be notified in a timely manner.

That is the ideal scenario. As we all know, the ideal does not always occur. Departures are not always amicable. So if the former firm will not agree or, more likely, delays sending a joint letter, it is permissible for the departing lawyer to send out a unilateral letter. If sending a unilateral letter, the departing lateral should copy the former firm on it.

ABA Formal Ethics Opinion 489 provides that if the law

firm and departing lawyer "cannot promptly agree on the terms of a joint letter, a law firm cannot prohibit the departing lawyer from soliciting firm clients." It also provides that "departing lawyers need not wait to inform clients of…their impending departure, provided that the firm is informed contemporaneously."

WHICH CLIENTS SHOULD BE NOTIFIED?

ABA Formal Ethics Opinion 99-414 defines "clients" who must receive notice of the departure as "clients for whose active matters the lawyer has direct professional responsibility at the time of the notice."

Opinion 99-414 provides that because she has a "present professional relationship with her current clients," she does not violate Model Rule 7.3 (solicitation prohibitions) by notifying those clients that she is leaving for a new firm.

Ultimately, if a joint notification letter is not practical or not possible, then the departing lawyer can notify "her current clients" on her own without any involvement from her current firm. However, she cannot do so with clients of the firm that are not considered her clients until *after* she has departed the current firm and joined the new firm. Additionally, as previously mentioned, if she sends a letter on her own notifying her clients, she should copy her old firm on the communication.

It is important to note here that under Rule 7.3, the departing lawyer cannot make in-person contact with firm clients with whom she does *not* have a prior professional or family relationship. There are some specific definitions around this. It is not enough for a lawyer to have worked on a matter for the client along with other lawyers if she had little or no direct contact with the client. This would be considered insufficient grounds for a "prior professional relationship," and the lawyer cannot make in-person contact with such a client.

What *does* count as a "prior professional relationship," you ask? As noted above, this would be the client whose active open matters the lawyer is currently handling, regardless of who originated the client.

GIVING NOTICE TO THE CURRENT FIRM

As for the actual process of notifying the current/soon-to-be prior firm, if you are a lawyer, I generally recommend that you give notice in person if at all possible. You should enter that meeting with a Notice of Withdrawal in final form, proposed joint notification letter, and client election document.

Finally, you should bring a list of any critical upcoming dates on client matters, as well as a plan for how all such dates can be met.

RECAP: DO'S AND DON'TS FOR DEPARTING LATERALS AND LAW FIRMS

If you are a lawyer thinking of moving to a better firm, consider this list of what you should and shouldn't do during your move.

As a departing lawyer, you should do the following:

1. Notify the current/soon-to-be former firm of your departure. As we just discussed, this needs to happen before notifying clients.
2. Communicate with clients. Tell them you are leaving. This must happen regardless of whether the prior firm will cooperate. You have an ethical obligation to keep your clients informed of relevant information, and, as their attorney, the

fact that you are changing firms is certainly relevant to them. A joint letter, sent with the prior firm, however, is best practice and should be attempted.

3. If the prior firm will not sign a joint letter, then you should send out a unilateral letter (and copy the prior firm) that explains the client's three options. A joint letter is preferred, but it is not required. Remember, your ethical priority is the client, and making sure they are not prejudiced or harmed in this lateral move.

4. The letter lists the client's three choices, which are as follows:
   A. The client can remain with the prior firm.
   B. The client can continue to be represented by you at your new firm.
   c. The client can seek different counsel altogether from a different lawyer and firm.

5. Continue your duties to the client as usual. If you are the attorney of record, then you handle client matters unless and until released by the court or terminated by the client. For example, let's say you give notice of departure on Tuesday and have a hearing for a client on Wednesday. You would handle that hearing and all other matters, unless and until released or terminated by the client.

6. Be fair and reasonable.

As a departing lawyer, you should not do the following:

1. Seek a client's commitment of legal work to the new firm *before* notifying the current/soon-to-be former firm of your intent to leave. You can ask relevant questions, such as whether a client has had any experience (good or bad) with a given law firm or whether the client has an opinion about a given law firm. That is not specifically precluded

under the ethical rules. However, asking whether a client's business would follow to a new firm *before notifying your prior firm* is not permissible.

A. Remove client files from your firm prior to giving notice and subsequently receiving the client's instructions. This includes electronic documents. The files belong to the client. By the same token, if the client's instructions are for you and your new firm to receive the files, then the prior firm should turn them over promptly.

B. Advise a client not to pay an existing bill or to pay you directly.

2. Compete with the old firm before departure by comparing services or rates of the two firms. Up until time of departure, you still owe fiduciary duties to the prior firm and its partners.

3. Malign the quality or price of the legal services of the prior firm. "Do not disparage" is a good rule for both you and your prior firm.

4. Solicit associates or other firm employees to leave with you prior to your actual departure. It should be noted that conversations with partners about potentially joining a lateral who is considering leaving are generally permissible. This is so because of the other partners' right to move. While associates and other employee attorneys also have the right to move, soliciting them to do so is considered a breach of fiduciary duty prior to the lateral's departure. Group moves of two or more partners is a practical result of partners being able to discuss making a lateral move together.

5. Conceal or delay taking on new clients or matters, with the intention that they would be handled entirely at the new firm.

6. Delay a settlement, or otherwise handle a litigation matter, so that it enhances the benefits of the new firm.

7. Use confidential and proprietary information of the prior firm.
8. Encourage clients to leave the prior firm.

Remember, if you plan to depart, you are still considered to be working for the former firm until you start with the new firm. You continue to owe the former firm fiduciary duties until your employment is terminated. You should continue to work, bill, and collect for your former firm right up until time of departure.

The current/former law firm also has principles it should follow. If you are a firm leader, use this as a guide in the event one of your partners decides to leave you.

The former/prior law firm should do the following:

1. Be reasonable. You have an obligation to be fair to the departing lateral. Not only is it a better approach to the situation, but also the client's interests are paramount. Being unreasonable about a departure can harm a client's interests. Not transferring client files quickly is an obvious example of being unreasonable, to the client's detriment.
2. Comply with the client's wishes. Whatever the client decides regarding overall representation and specific matters and files, the former/prior firm should adhere to the decision in a reasonably timely manner.

The former/prior law firm should not do the following:

1. Prevent the departing lawyer from honoring her ethical obligations to clients, or attempt to thwart any ongoing relationship between that lawyer and departing clients by, for example, disallowing the lawyer from accessing firm resources to service clients. Let the departing lawyer con-

duct business as usual in servicing her clients. The clients' needs are paramount.

2. Forbid a departing lawyer from announcing her departure, notifying clients, or opposing counsel in a litigated matter. After the departing lawyer has notified you and your firm, she has an obligation to notify other interested parties, especially her clients.

3. Instruct firm personnel not to disclose the whereabouts of former lawyers to clients or other callers. It is not reasonable to withhold such information.

4. Withhold files of departing clients as leverage in disputes with the departing lawyer over fees or other strictly lawyer-to-lawyer issues. This is a big one. The files belong to the client.

5. Disparage the departing lawyer or her new firm. This is common sense and basic professionalism.

CHAPTER 10

DUE DILIGENCE

WE HAVE GONE OVER A LOT OF RULES AND PROCEDURES, but all of this information is critically important if you are a law firm leader or a lawyer considering a lateral move. Now let's talk about another important area, one that is essential to every lateral hiring situation: due diligence. Due diligence refers to the process of gathering relevant information prior to conducting a significant transaction.

In a lateral hiring situation, both the hiring firm and the prospective lateral need to conduct thorough due diligence on the other prior to the offer and acceptance stages. While no amount of due diligence can guarantee success, the better and more thorough the parties are in the due diligence process, the greater the chances of a successful lateral hire.

Here is some helpful advice for both firm leaders and prospective laterals.

DUE DILIGENCE BY THE HIRING (NEW) FIRM

So, you are the leader of a hiring firm. Due diligence means learning as much as you can about the prospective lateral prior to hiring her into your firm.

In addition to quantitative data, which is mainly provided by the Lateral Partner Questionnaire (LPQ), your firm should thoroughly review qualitative factors as part of its due diligence process. What were the reasons the lateral made moves in the past? Has she been consistent in her stated reasons for wanting to make a lateral move now? Is she a good cultural fit? Does she understand the hiring firm's culture and how it differs from her current firm's?

Also, be sure to analyze the prospective lateral's business plan. This is an important part of the due diligence process. A good business plan should explain the lawyer's practice and the clients she has developed to date. More importantly, it should explain in detail her plan for growing her practice, and how she can leverage the resources of your firm to expand her client base and the services that can be provided to her existing clients.

You should also analyze readily available information such as court filings, transactions records, academic transcripts (from the lateral), industry and commercial media, and social media feeds. Your firm should also check references, but only if it can be done discreetly. Otherwise, this should be done after an offer has been accepted so that confidentiality is maintained for the lateral.

The bottom line is that gathering more relevant information increases the odds of conducting a lateral hire that is successful for both the firm and the lateral.

Now, let's go over this process in detail.

GET CLEAR ON THE LATERAL CANDIDATE'S PORTABLE BUSINESS

If you are hiring, most likely you believe the lateral can bring portable business with her. Naturally, you will want to learn as much as you can about the lateral's personal and professional background, her clients, and the business she will be bringing with her. Do *not* hire a lateral unless you have learned enough about her to conclude that hiring her would be a sound business move and would yield a good return on your investment.

Importantly, as we previously discussed, there are ethical issues with the gathering of this information because much of it can be considered confidential. She cannot breach her fiduciary duties to her current partners, and you certainly do not want to be seen as encouraging any such breach.

How do you learn what you need to know and still remain on the right side of any ethical issues?

First, learn the identities of the lateral's clients. This is not considered confidential information. In fact, many firms list their clients on their websites. Moreover, as stated previously, courts have made a distinction between the clients an attorney has closely worked with and those that are firm clients with whom the attorney has had little or no contact.

Thus, there should not be any issues with the lateral identifying her clients. As a part of client identification, the lateral should be able to provide contact names and information. However, these individuals should *not* be contacted before the lateral has notified her current firm that she is leaving. Moreover, you should inform the lateral not to print out any client lists or contact information from her current firm's internal systems.

Of course, you will want to know more than just the names and contact information of the lateral's clients. A good rule of thumb is to seek only the information necessary to assess the lateral's practice and the financial information related to her practice, but nothing beyond this.

Stated differently, the lateral should be able to provide information regarding her representation of specific clients as it pertains to billings, collections, and bill rates. However, she should not provide information that goes beyond the details of her relationship with the client—especially information regarding her current firm's relationship that goes beyond her own.

Moreover, do not ask for or accept any documents that have been generated or produced from the lateral's current firm. Common examples would be internally produced or computer-generated printouts of clients lists (unless this list is publicly available, as on a website), client contact information, billing information, compensation information, and the like. Many firms explicitly state on their LPQ that they do not want any documents generated from the lateral's current firm. This is a good protective statement to put on your firm's LPQ, and one that we recommend.

AVOID ASSOCIATE AND STAFF INFORMATION

Just do not ask for this. If the lateral wants to bring associates, paralegals, practice assistants, or other staff with her, you should not ask for names, salaries, and billing rates of those individuals. The lateral may volunteer those names, and probably will, but you as the hiring firm should not specifically ask for those names. Similarly, do not accept any documents or lists with the names of associates, paralegals, or other staff already printed on them.

PERFORM CONFLICTS DUE DILIGENCE

As mentioned previously, it is generally not a problem for the lateral to disclose the names of her clients for conflicts purposes. However, neither the lateral's clients nor the hiring firm's clients should be contacted about potential conflicts before notice is given to the lateral's current firm. In other words, internal conflict checks can be done, but *do not* communicate with clients before notice is given to her current firm.

ADMINISTER LATERAL PARTNER QUESTIONNAIRES

Also called the LPQ, the Lateral Partner Questionnaire is a foundational component of due diligence. LPQs not only provide the hiring firm with vital information, but, if drafted properly, they can also establish the ground rules with the lateral under consideration. Assuming it is well crafted, the LPQ will ask about the prospective lateral's clients, originations, rates, production, collections, compensation (where permitted), employment history, educational history, disciplinary history, malpractice history, and relevant aspects of personal history such as bankruptcies and criminal background.

Although most LPQs are similar, the best ones advise the lateral that the hiring firm is not asking for, nor does it want, any confidential information from her current firm. Next, they advise the lateral that she should not engage in any solicitation of clients or employees of her current firm unless and until she has given notice of her departure.

Finally, your LPQ should focus on what the lateral anticipates will happen when she joins the hiring firm. In other words, the hiring firm will want to know—and the LPQ should ask for—what she reasonably expects will come with the lateral as far as business volume, types of matters, complementary practice areas, and the type of support she will need.

This is all good and reasonable. Make sure the LPQ does *not* ask for historical records of billings, collections, rates, names of key staff, and the like, as those records *may* be considered proprietary to the lateral's current firm.

ASK FOR ADDITIONAL INFORMATION

Hiring law firms typically ask for additional information, none of which creates ethical issues as long as it is not produced by the current law firm and does not contain confidential information. Some suggestions for what you can ask from your lateral candidate include the following:

- a business plan
- tax returns
- certificates of good standing with the Bar
- background checks (formal and informal)
- reference checks (at the end of the process, usually after notice has been given)

DUE DILIGENCE BY THE PROSPECTIVE LATERAL

If you are a prospective lateral, due diligence means learning as much as you can about the hiring law firm.

Although it is not discussed nearly as often, due diligence on the hiring firm by the lateral is also vitally important. Your career is literally at stake. You need to learn as much as you can about the law firm, its culture, financial strengths and weaknesses (e.g., revenue, debt, collection issues), governance model, leaders, strategies, compensation system, clients, the compensation range of its partners, its business development tactics and methods, its resources, its history of lateral hires and departures, and more.

Much of this information is obviously sensitive and confidential, and few firms will be willing to disclose it during the early stages of recruitment. So, as a prospective lateral, you need to realize that firms will probably disclose information in stages. As talks progress, and the lateral shares more information, and the parties appear to be more serious about working together, the more information the firm should be willing to disclose.

Additionally, you should spend some time with current, and especially former, lawyers of the firm. What was it like to work there? What were the pros and cons? There is no substitute for speaking to individuals who have experienced what you are considering doing.

Certainly, confidentiality concerns are a major consideration and make the due diligence process more difficult for laterals. Nevertheless, before you accept an offer, and certainly before you notify your current firm and inform your clients of your departure, if you are a wise lateral, you will have done your homework on exactly what type of firm you will be joining.

Common Mistakes by Law Firms and Laterals

CHAPTER 11

EIGHTEEN MISTAKES LAW FIRMS FREQUENTLY MAKE IN LATERAL HIRING

IF YOU ARE A FIRM LEADER, THIS CHAPTER IS FOR YOU. **The best, most efficient way for law firms to grow is through lateral hiring.** It is infinitely faster than organic growth. If you want to grow your firm, the only other option is lateral hiring, whether by individuals, firms, or groups, because at a certain point, lawyers simply have no more capacity to add work to their plates. Therefore, growing your firm will require adding lawyers, and that means lateral hiring.

However, as a firm leader, having an interest in lateral hiring does not guarantee success. There are numerous mistakes firms frequently make in their lateral hiring efforts. I will explain the eighteen most common mistakes in this chapter.

1. NOT HAVING A PLAN TO GROW

In my 20-plus years of working with law firms, the biggest strategic mistake I have seen firms make is not having a plan to grow at all. Growing a law firm, like growing any business entity, takes effort. It takes planning. It takes having the infrastructure and framework to support a plan. And it takes the willingness to implement the plan.

In other words, growth does not just happen. Law firm leaders have to actively pursue growth as a key objective of the firm, second only to profitability. Law firm leaders must have a plan and then execute on it.

Unfortunately, many law firm leaders, especially of smaller and midsize firms, do not view growth as a strategic objective that must be implemented. They view it as an occurrence outside of their control: growth either happens or it does not. The firm either has enough work to warrant hiring additional lawyers or it does not. The laterals with the large books either join us or they do not.

This view typically does not extend more than a year into the future, two years at the most. For the next one or two years, things might look fine. The firm has plenty of work, and the lawyers are all busy. Revenues and profits are up.

Let's say this is your firm. On the surface, there is nothing inherently wrong with this type of short-term, nonchalant approach. After all, many firms like their current size and do not want to get any bigger. They are certainly not worried about what is going to happen years down the road.

The problem is that it is nearly impossible to maintain the status quo for any long period of time. Instead of maintaining the firm's current size, eventually the firm begins to shrink. Lawyers retire; they die unexpectedly; they make lateral moves to other firms. The lawyers who remain get older. You find yourself in a situation where lawyers who are over age 65 or 70 control the majority of the firm's revenues and clients. Meanwhile, there are few obvious successors for these clients and this business.

Before you know it, your headcount is 20 percent less than what you thought was the "ideal size" for your firm. Even worse, now your firm is viewed as stagnant in the market. You are considered an "old firm." You decide you should actually add some strong laterals with good books of business.

Unfortunately, you are no longer recruiting from a position of strength. You are considered a weaker player in the market, a stagnant firm. This makes the challenge of attracting laterals much more difficult. This means either you have to take weaker lawyers as lateral hires or you have to pay a premium to get the laterals you want.

If you do not do these things—and sometimes even if you do—your firm cannot escape the downward spiral of diminishing revenues and profits and shrinking headcount. Current clients notice. Prospective clients are certain to hear about your issues from your competitors. It can become an impossible situation that may ultimately sink your firm. And it all started because your firm did not make and execute upon a deliberate plan to grow.

2. FORGETTING THAT THE FIRM IS A SELLER AS WELL AS A BUYER

Another very common mistake firms make when they want to grow is they forget they are selling as well as buying. In other words, they forget they are recruiting laterals to join their firm (selling) in addition to hiring expensive new employees or partners (buying). Many firms have a tendency to focus on the latter to the neglect of the former.

To an extent, this makes sense. A lateral partner is a major investment. Strong laterals are typically very expensive. They command high compensation, benefits, marketing resources, office space, staff, and other costs. There are often expensive search fees as part of the transaction.

A new hire is a disruption. It takes time away from management and staff in order to properly integrate the lateral and any other lawyers or staff she may bring with her. Thus, it is natural for firms to want to act as cautious buyers. In fact, firms should act as cautious buyers. Due diligence is vital and must be done, which we discussed previously.

The mistake occurs when firms become so focused on their due diligence and their role as a cautious buyer that they *neglect their role as an enthusiastic seller*. That is, they do not adequately sell their firms to the lateral.

Firms are well advised to put themselves in the lateral's shoes. When we work with law firm clients, we advise them to remember the lateral candidate experience (LCE). When a lateral is considering a move to your firm, she will be impacted by every element of her experience, from how she is greeted by the receptionist to compensation negotiations and everything in between. It is not an overstatement to say that her LCE will largely determine whether she joins your firm.

Most laterals, by definition, are in an attractive situation. They are usually practicing with a strong firm and typically have a book of business ranging from adequate to enormous. They are only considering your firm because most intelligent professionals, especially in our current age of free agency, are willing to consider what may be an even better opportunity. Your firm's job is to convince laterals why your firm is better for them and their practice. Recruiting is selling.

Hiring a lateral is not like hiring most employees. For most employees, the hiring entity has an opening. Candidates express interest and try to convince the entity why they are the best fit for the position, and one of them is hired.

Lateral attorneys, on the other hand, are not looking for a job. They have a job, and it is usually a very good job. Would a position with your firm be even better? Again, that is the view you must sell.

In addition, firms need to be mindful that their fiercest competitors may also want this lateral. Generally speaking, firms want the same types of laterals. The criteria may change a bit, but usually not a lot. If your firm is not willing to be humble enough to sell the firm's attributes to a valuable prospective lateral, your competitors certainly will be.

On a related note, some think their firms sell themselves. They believe their firm name and reputation are so lofty that any lateral would want to work there. They believe their firm can pick and choose the laterals they want and do not have to do any actual selling.

There may be firms that have such tremendous reputations and high profits per equity partner (PEPs) that the firm literally recruits itself, but in my experience, those are *extremely* rare. Unless your firm is one of those very few, you will need to recruit if you want to add strong laterals.

Yes, your firm's name and reputation are strengths. But arrogance is a weakness—one your competitors will gladly exploit.

3. NOT HAVING A COMPELLING REASON

Related to the mistake of not selling the firm, another common mistake is not providing laterals with a compelling reason to join the firm. This is essential.

What type of compelling reason? There are many, and it

will, of course, vary by firm and even by practice area, but a few reasons include the following:

- a larger footprint
- more practice areas to offer clients
- deeper bench
- greater rate autonomy
- reputation of the firm overall that directly benefits the lateral's practice
- reputation of the firm's expertise in the lateral's practice area
- greater compensation in the short term and/or long term

These are only a few examples. The point is that the lateral needs a strong reason to want to make the move to your firm. It is much easier for the lateral to stay in his current firm because change is usually difficult.

When we work with law firms, one of our very first questions is "Why should a lateral make a move to your firm?" If the firm does not have good answers to this question, we recommend they take the time to come up with several good answers before the lateral recruiting process even begins. After all, if the firm itself cannot state why a lateral should join them, then a good lateral probably will not be able to think of a reason to join them either.

4. MOVING TOO SLOWLY

As mentioned previously, one of the most frustrating impediments to lateral hiring and law firm growth is when the firm moves too slowly with the process. Timing and momentum are critical elements in lateral hiring. It is difficult to bring a strong, qualified lateral to the table for a law firm to consider. If it were easy, search firms would not be able to charge high fees. Once a prospective lateral is engaged, the hiring firm must be willing and able to move through the process at a deliberate pace.

To be clear, I am not suggesting that firms skip proper due diligence or that they should not follow their established lateral hiring process (and firms should have one). I *am* suggesting that firms should execute the steps of the process without needless delay.

The lateral hiring process is just that: it is a process with specific steps. Some delays between steps are natural, such as when the hiring partner is in a trial and will be out of pocket for two weeks. Everyone understands that, assuming, of course, this information is relayed to the lateral.

What is less understandable is when the process seems to be delayed for no apparent reason. When a lateral candidate looks strong on paper (large book, good rates, etc.) and agrees to be submitted to a firm for consideration, the firm needs to move on her quickly. I suggest a response time of 72 hours or less. Any longer than a week is problematic.

Good laterals know their value in the market. If a lateral agrees to be submitted and then a week or longer goes by with no word from the firm, the lateral starts to conclude the firm is not interested. That lateral, of course, has pride and an ego (as we all do), and pretty soon she will conclude she does not want to interview with that firm anyway.

Let's say our slow-moving law firm finally gets around to reviewing the lateral's information and, of course, decides they would love to meet with her. But it is too late. The lateral has already withdrawn from consideration—all because the firm moved too slowly.

This scenario can happen at almost any stage of the process. I have seen it happen too many times after a first meeting or interview. After the first interview, both sides are excited. There seem to be synergies, and both sides can see a lot of growth potential between the firm's platform and the lateral's practice. The lateral is already thinking about next steps.

However, the firm does nothing. A week goes by. Two weeks go by. No action steps are taken, and the lateral's thoughts become influenced by pride and ego. Perhaps the firm remains interested in the lateral. They are just not in any hurry. But momentum subsides. And many times, the firm loses.

The bottom line is that *time kills deals.* Yes, there are exceptions, and we discuss a few of those later in this chapter. But generally speaking, the longer a deal drags on, the less likely it is to close.

5. BEING DISORGANIZED

It is critical that firms are organized when it comes to lateral hiring. Organization is so important because the lateral hiring process revolves around people, and people are complex. The lateral hiring process itself is fairly straightforward, but it inevitably involves many complications due to the human element.

A lateral hire is an investment. It is an asset purchase, but unlike buying an object or an entity, with a lateral hire, you are dealing with people. People can be emotional, sensitive, and sometimes illogical. People have egos, opinions, and all of the other complications that go along with human beings. The relevance of all of these human factors is they make the process complicated.

The best way to manage a complicated process is to have an organized plan for its execution. Unfortunately, truly organized firms are the exception rather than the rule when it comes to lateral hiring.

As noted in Chapter 7, it is strongly recommended to put one person in charge of the process of hiring each specific lateral. That one person should have a comprehensive checklist to follow, which lists every step. This will greatly help eliminate the disorganization that is so frequently found in law firm lateral hiring.

Otherwise, questions like these are sure to arise: Who at the firm should receive the initial submission of the lateral's bio and information? Is there one point person, or does it vary? If it is one person, does that person have time to deal with potential laterals? Does that person have a lateral hiring committee he or she reports to, or perhaps he or she leads that committee? Once that initial step has been handled, how does the firm move forward? Who is responsible for communications with the lateral? Who schedules the meetings? Who meets with the lateral on behalf of the firm?

After meetings with the lateral, who is responsible for the due diligence? Who is responsible for the LPQ? What if the lateral has specific questions about the firm and/or the relevant practice group? What about cross-selling opportunities? Who manages the conflicts checks?

If the firm is organized, it has a specific process in place to handle all of these questions and issues, and it has one professional who is ultimately accountable. Depending on the size of the firm, this one person may have a team who helps her, and those team members may be responsible for different specific steps in the process, or for different individual laterals, but ultimately she is accountable. If the firm is not so organized, it is easy to see how the lateral hiring process can become bogged down. That, of course, causes delays, and that is usually when the firm loses good laterals.

6. HAVING TOO MANY MEETINGS

A common mistake among firms that are somewhat inexperienced with lateral hiring is asking the prospective lateral to attend too many meetings. This is understandable. When firms are relatively new to the lateral hiring process, they want to get as many partners involved as possible. Hiring a lateral is a significant investment. Rather than getting out too far in front of the team, firm leaders want others to be involved.

On the surface, there is nothing wrong with this mindset. It becomes a problem, however, when the lateral is asked to attend five, six, or seven meetings all for the purpose of meeting more lawyers in the firm. This can be a turnoff for strong laterals who have options in the market.

Attending these meetings is something of a burden. It is time consuming. There is a certain amount of preparation work the lateral needs to do (or at least should do). Plus, every meeting increases the risk that the lateral's current firm will find out about the lateral's interest in leaving, which is obviously a concern for most laterals.

Rather than subjecting the lateral to multiple meetings solely for the purpose of meeting more people, it is better for you, the firm leader, to take a much more structured approach along the following lines:

The first step is a meeting with a small number of people, usually some of the leadership of the firm. Perhaps this is the hiring partner and one or two relevant practice group leaders.

Assuming that goes well, the second step widens the circle. This is the meeting at which the firm leaders who have not previously met the lateral will meet him. Additionally, a certain percentage of the general firm partnership should meet the prospective lateral.

The third step is sometimes a social event, but it does not

have to be. This is a chance for any partners who would like to meet (or meet again) with the lateral to do so. If partners are not able to meet with the lateral during the second or third meeting, then they have to trust their partners who believe the lateral would be a good addition.

And that is it. Three meetings. Four at the outside. Not every single partner or partner in that office is going to be able to meet every single lateral. It is overly burdensome to ask the lateral to attend more than three or four such meetings, absent some particular reason to do so. For example, if there are potential or actual conflicts, or relevant deadlines or pressing business development opportunities that warrant additional meetings, then of course those should happen. Otherwise, firms should endeavor to limit these meetings.

Note the steps above only pertain to meetings. They do not include the other relevant steps, such as conflicts checks and LPQs. As it pertains to "get acquainted" meetings, however, firms are making a mistake if they ask a lateral for more than three, or four at the most.

7. EXPECTING LATERALS TO TAKE A PAY CUT

No matter how great your firm is, asking a good lateral to take a pay cut in order to join your firm usually results in that lateral *not* joining your firm. Good laterals have too many other options in today's market.

There are a couple of reasons law firms make the mistake of asking a lateral to take a pay cut when trying to add talent to their firms.

The first reason is an overinflated sense of the firm's stature (see Mistake #2 in this chapter). This is related to the mistake of believing they do not have to sell to recruits because their firm is so prestigious that any lawyer would want to work there. As it relates to compensation, some firms cling to the belief that laterals should be willing to take a pay cut in order to work at their firm. This is simply a mistake.

This is not a knock at any firm. Most of the firms we work with are outstanding, and they present excellent opportunities to their lawyers and prospective laterals. That does not mean, however, that the firms are so prominent that laterals will be willing to reduce their compensation in order to work there. That is simply asking too much of the lateral.

The second reason is the firm's compensation system is structured so that the candidate will have to "prove herself" in order to make her current compensation, much less anything above that. While such a compensation system is understandable from the perspective of the firm, most good laterals simply will not do it. There are too many other good firms that will not impose this type of burden on the prospective lateral.

As shocking as this might be to read, I have yet to meet an attorney who wanted to take a pay cut in my 20-plus years of working as a consultant to lawyers and law firms.

In other words, if you want to grow your firm by adding lateral talent, then you need to be prepared to pay for that talent, absent some unusual situation. I am not suggesting "buying lawyers" or overpaying for them. In fact, that is another mistake that will be addressed later in this section. But the bottom line is that if you want to add talent to your firm, you need to understand that talented lawyers are usually not going to take a pay cut to join you.

8. NOT HAVING A STRATEGY

So, you want to grow your firm? It is important to know *why*. What is the purpose? Is it focused on a particular market or practice area? Is it to expand offerings to existing clients? Is it to strengthen the firm's reputation in a particular industry?

There are numerous valid reasons. In fact, simply adding headcount and creating a deeper bench is a perfectly fine reason. Get clear on yours, though, because it will dictate your growth strategy.

Without a solid strategy, a firm's chances of success in adding lateral talent become much lower.

9. NOT KNOWING YOUR FIRM'S MAIN SELLING POINTS

Firms have to truly know themselves before they can attract the right lateral talent.

All firms are different. They have different cultures, different systems, and different strengths and weaknesses. They have different selling points, and in order to effectively recruit top laterals (i.e., sell their firm to laterals), they have to know which selling points their firm can actually employ.

This begins with an honest, in-depth evaluation of the firm. All firms, like every business entity, should conduct a SWOT analysis. This is a comprehensive, detailed analysis of the firm's strengths, weaknesses, opportunities, and threats. Only by truly understanding its strengths in the market can a firm know what selling points will resonate the most with prospective laterals.

Of course, these selling points must be genuine and must correlate to the true strengths of the firm. A firm cannot sell itself as having a broad, robust IP practice if there are only two lawyers in the firm who do any IP work, for example.

An equally important aspect of the SWOT analysis is that it

also reveals the firm's weaknesses. As a firm leader, this provides you with a list of items to be improved. It also enables the firm to prepare talking points to address these weaknesses when prospective laterals raise them during interviews.

10. NOT UNDERSTANDING YOUR FIRM'S REAL NEEDS

Many law firms make the mistake of entering the lateral attorney market without truly understanding what they actually need. For example, I have had firms tell me they have an overabundance of work and need an experienced lawyer to help them handle the overflow. Fair enough. That is a good problem to have.

The mistake arises when we begin to discuss the specific criteria for what they want in a lateral, and they tell me the lawyer they hire for this position must have a full, self-sustaining book of business. Then I begin to ask questions like this:

"Well, if the lateral has a full, self-sustaining book of business, *how* is he going to help your firm with its overflow of work? There are only so many hours in a day. How can the lateral service his own clients while also helping with the overflow of work from your clients if he has a full book of business?

"Furthermore, if the lateral has a full, self-sustaining book of business, *why* is he going to help your firm with its overflow of work? What is the benefit to the lateral? No lawyer is going to stop working for his own clients in order to do work for your clients.

"If you have an overflow of work, and you need a good lawyer to help you get the work done, why does the lateral need to have a full book of business? I can understand the firm wanting the lateral to have some business, as it demonstrates an ability to actually develop clients and generate revenue, but why must he have a full book if the firm needs the lateral to take on an overflow of existing work in the firm?"

Similarly, I have had law firm clients tell me they could bring in a significant amount of business if they only had a good, experienced rainmaker who could combine his business development acumen with their relationships. In other words, they can open the doors, but they need someone to walk into the room and help them close some business.

This presents the same problems as the previous scenario. Certainly, the hiring law firm wants confirmation that the lateral in question knows how to close business, and the best way to verify this ability is with a proven track record. However, some firms will insist on any such lateral having a full, self-sustaining book of business before being hired for such a role.

The same type of questions arise: "If the lateral has a full, self-sustaining book of business, how is he going to have the time to help close these business opportunities? Moreover, why will the lateral want to do this if his plate is full with his own clients?"

We encourage our law firm clients to think about what they truly need. In the two previous scenarios, our advice would be to hire a good lawyer with some business, but not a full book. Hire a good lawyer whose plate is approximately half-full and who is hungry to help bring in more business. This is a much more feasible option for the above scenarios and is more in line with what the firm truly needs.

11. HIRING LATERALS WHO ARE BAD FITS

Truly successful firms understand their culture. They understand their firm, their various practices, their expertise, and where they fit within the legal marketplace. Unfortunately, some firms do not have this understanding. They attempt to grow by hiring laterals who are poor fits, and it almost never works. Or worse, it works, the lateral is hired (at great expense), and the mismatch becomes evident only later. Eventually, the lateral leaves the firm.

What makes a lawyer a bad fit? It could be a number of factors, but the most common ones are incompatible practice areas, significant discrepancy with rates, different expectations as far as hours billed, different expectations as far as originations expected, excessive conflicts, differences over staff requirements, differences over resources, different opinions regarding overhead, very difficult personalities, and, of course, different beliefs and expectations over compensation and compensation structures. If a prospective lateral does not view these factors in the same general light as the law firm, that is a major red flag that the lateral is a poor fit for the firm, regardless of her numbers.

12. SOLE RELIANCE ON NUMBERS (DISREGARDING COMMON SENSE)

It is true that numbers are a critical component of any lateral hire. Arguably, the most important number when a firm is considering a lateral is that lateral's portable book of business. The first question asked is almost always "What can she bring to the table?" In other words, how much business/revenue/client base will this lateral bring in the door if we hire her?

Most good law firms will have a general minimum book requirement, as in "Do not bring us a candidate with less than $800,000," or whatever that firm's minimum amount is.

The problem arises when firms become so focused on current numbers and the past three years' historical numbers that they miss enormous opportunities. This does not happen often, but when it does, it is a huge mistake.

I once worked with a lateral whose book of business was approximately $250,000. This was considerably below my client's minimum book requirement. Normally, I would not have presented this candidate because he did not meet the criteria. However, there was an outlier with this candidate—an additional factor that was much more important than his current book amount.

Because of an easily verified relationship, he had the ability to generate well over $1 million in legal fees, and probably more on an annual basis. Why did he not have the business in hand currently? His current firm did not have the expertise or bandwidth to service this client. In fact, that was the main reason this lawyer wanted to make a lateral move. Plus, he liked my client's platform, broad array of services, rate structure, and reputation.

Unfortunately, my client could not get past the fact that this lateral did not have an existing book over $750,000, their general minimum book requirement. They were unwilling to "take the risk" on the lateral, despite my best efforts to convince them otherwise. This was, of course, a significant mistake.

The lateral ended up joining another firm. At last count, his annual business from this one client alone was almost $2 million. The firm he joined took a risk, arguably, but it was small and it paid off.

I am not saying you should lack minimum standards, nor am I saying you should take reckless chances on laterals. I *am* saying that sometimes common sense is more important than numbers and historical data. This is particularly true for firms that are struggling to attract the talent they need. Sometimes, common sense tells you to take a chance, and more often than not, it is a chance worth taking.

13. NOT HAVING FIRM LEADERSHIP INVOLVED

A common characteristic of firms that struggle to attract lateral talent is not having firm leadership involved in the lateral hiring process. Leaders at such firms tend to stay removed from it. They rarely make themselves available to meet with laterals. If they do meet, these leaders spend the bare minimum amount of time with them. They do not prioritize lateral recruiting as a strategic objective for the firm. In a nutshell, they view lateral hiring as a chore that others in the firm need to handle.

On the contrary, the firms experiencing the most success in lateral hiring usually have the active involvement of firm leadership. The Managing Partner of the firm is often one of the first, if not the very first, contacts for top lateral talent. This sends the message to a lateral that she is important. She matters. This is powerful and can make all the difference.

As mentioned before, I would advise you to keep a point person—such as a Chief Talent Officer—who is accountable for making the hiring process run smoothly. Ideally, this is not a lawyer. Lawyers need to be involved, but they do not need to be managing the important yet time-consuming activities that are involved in lateral hiring. For a busy lawyer with clients to serve, it is too easy to put recruiting activities on the back burner. This is what leads to frustrated laterals and an unsuccessful lateral hiring program.

I have experienced the consequences of not allowing access to firm leadership myself, as an advisor, which ultimately harmed the firm. Once, we had a client in a good legal market that was serious about their desire to grow by acquiring lateral talent. The problem was that this firm utterly refused to allow us access to the decision-makers and influencers in the firm.

This severely hindered our ability to do the job. Not only could we not develop critical information we needed, such as the reasons certain promising laterals were being rejected (obviously crucial in order to avoid repeating the same issue), but our prospective laterals were also denied this access.

Prospective laterals have questions, often ones that need to be answered by firm leaders and practice group leaders, and they want access to these leaders. It shows prospective laterals they are important to the law firm. When that access is denied and those questions are not sufficiently addressed, the prospective laterals usually withdraw from consideration.

In our situation, the roadblock we had was caused by the firm's internal recruiting professionals. Whether it was insecurity, a turf war, or internal politics we will never know, but it was unfortunate because it cost this firm a substantial amount of talent and revenue.

14. LACK OF COMMITMENT TO LATERAL HIRING

A quite common mistake we see firms make is taking a lackadaisical approach to lateral hiring. These firms make lateral hiring a secondary priority (or less). They view it as something to work on after their other priorities have been addressed.

The problem with this approach is that it makes success in lateral hiring much less likely. If a firm wants to add top-level talent, it has to make recruiting a high priority for the firm. Period. Otherwise, it will not achieve its objectives for growth.

If a law firm is not comfortable recruiting on its own or does not have the expertise or bandwidth, then that law firm should hire a reputable attorney search firm to add lateral talent. Otherwise, growth will not happen. Without a deliberate plan for growth and the execution of such a plan, it will be nearly impossible for a firm to add the talent it wants.

15. NOT BEING PATIENT WITH LATERALS

Without a doubt, I believe in taking an active, aggressive approach when it comes to lateral hiring. Competition is fierce, and the aggressive execution of a good plan is the right way to handle lateral hiring.

However, there are times when the right move is to slow down, sometimes even to the point of doing nothing. There will be situations in which a good lateral is seriously interested in a law firm, but for various reasons, she cannot make the move right now.

Sometimes these reasons are professional, such as a conflict that needs to be resolved. Sometimes the delay is unavoidable due to a personal matter. Sometimes the reasons are financial. For example, perhaps the lateral cannot leave her current firm before a certain date because she will be receiving a large distribution or bonus on that date.

Usually, as previously mentioned, time is the enemy of lateral hiring. But whether professional or personal, there are sometimes occasions when a prospective lateral simply needs some time. If the lateral is sincere and open about the reasons for the delay, and the firm trusts what the lateral is saying about it, then giving the lateral the time to work through issues can be the right move and can be the difference between success and failure.

16. NOT MAINTAINING CONFIDENTIALITY

If there is a cardinal rule in the world of lateral hiring, it is this: the prospective lateral's candidacy must be held in strict confidence at all times, period. Violating this rule is not only highly unprofessional and a severe breach of trust, but it also can doom a firm's chances of success in hiring good laterals.

When lateral prospects are exploring other opportunities, 99 percent of the time they are doing so without the knowledge of their current firm. This means that lateral hiring is an endeavor that is confidential per se.

To be clear, the overwhelming majority of firms and lawyers understand and respect this, and they maintain strict confidentiality. After all, nearly every professional has at some point in his or her career explored other opportunities and gone on interviews for those opportunities. Consequently, nearly every professional understands the sensitivity of the situation and acts accordingly.

It only takes one person, however, to blow up the entire process for a given lateral. If one person in a law firm breaches confidentiality, even by accident, the results can be disastrous for the lateral and problematic for the law firm.

17. BUYING LAWYERS

Through the years, a number of firms have made the fatal mistake of "buying lawyers." By that, I am referring to the practice of significantly overpaying for lateral talent with lengthy guarantees. To land lateral talent, these firms paid substantially more than the lawyers were worth according to standard metrics, and their compensation was guaranteed for a number of years.

Not only did this practice cause severe economic damage to some firms, but it actually helped put a number of them out of business. Some of these firms were among the largest and most prestigious law firms in the world at the time.

These firms often had to take on substantial debt to pay the exorbitant, guaranteed salaries. Furthermore, the law firms angered their existing partners who had contributed greatly to the firms' success for years but whose compensation was much lower than many of the new laterals' compensation. Additionally, theirs was not guaranteed. In sum, it was a recipe for disaster.

To be clear, law firms have to pay for lateral talent. On occasion, law firms have to pay a premium to land the lateral talent they really want to acquire, and sometimes that requires a guarantee of a year or even two on rare occasions. However, when law firms pay compensation that is well above what a lawyer is worth on the open market, and when that compensation is guaranteed for three, four, or five years, it is a major mistake that can cause significant harm to and even the dissolution of the firm.

18. INSUFFICIENT DUE DILIGENCE

Conducting due diligence is such a critical part of the lateral hiring process that we devoted an entire chapter to it. You can refer back to Chapter 10 for an in-depth analysis.

CHAPTER 12

SEVENTEEN MISTAKES LAWYERS FREQUENTLY MAKE IN MANAGING THEIR CAREERS

IF YOU ARE A LAWYER IN THE 21ST CENTURY, THEN YOU are a free agent. This is the gig economy, meaning people have more ability than ever to work for themselves and manage their careers. While you may not be able to control your own hours the way an Uber driver or a Shipt shopper can, you have more control over your career than ever before. In addition to the fact that lawyers get to choose whichever practice areas they wish to pursue, lawyers with the right credentials and clients have an almost endless number of options for where they can practice.

Despite these facts, many lawyers do a poor job of managing their careers. Instead of a career that grows with better clients, higher rates, more sophisticated legal work, and greater income, too many lawyers' careers become stagnant or, even worse, decline over time. To have a career of growth and success, avoid the following common mistakes lawyers make over the course of their careers.

1. NOT HAVING A PLAN TO GROW

The biggest mistake we see with lawyers is that they barely think of their careers at all. Many talented attorneys end up in positions for which they are overqualified and underpaid, and with which they are generally unhappy. If you ask them how they ended up in such a position, they will invariably say they were "too busy" to think about their careers. They were simply working away, and before they realized it, the years and opportunities had slipped by.

A career has to be managed. It has to be directed. It has to be nurtured. Mostly, it has to be planned, and then the plan(s) must be executed.

Like many ambitious people, you need to realize that the universe does not care how busy you are. It does not care how many jury trials you try or how many deals you close. No one is coming to guide your career path for you. There is only one person who can steer your career where it should go. If you have not taken the time to figure out where you want to go with your career, then chances are that you will not be happy with its final destination.

More than almost any other profession, lawyers have innumerable options for what they can do with their careers. Even within specific practice areas, there are countless options for an effective lawyer with good clients and experience.

But if this is the case, then why do some lawyers' careers always seem to be getting better while others' seem to be perpetually stuck? The ones whose careers are ascendant have taken the time to figure out where they want to be and have executed a plan to get there. They are proactive with their careers rather than reactive.

Sometimes, successful execution of a legal career requires a total career change. Sometimes it does not. Sometimes it entails a move in-house—or not. Most commonly, sometimes the successful execution of a legal career plan requires a lateral move, or more than one lateral move, over the course of a 40-plus-year career. Regardless, the most successful lawyers are the ones who have taken the time to figure out what they want to do, what they want to achieve, and where they want to be, and then have created a plan to get them there.

2. NOT MOVING WHEN IT IS TIME TO MOVE

I am in the business of helping law firms grow by lateral acquisition. This means I am generally in favor of lawyers moving from Firm A to Firm B, assuming it makes business sense for the firm and the lateral. Nevertheless, there are certainly times when changing firms is not the right move for the lateral. As professionals, my team and I always strive to give honest advice and feedback to the lawyers with whom we work. We present the pros and cons, and try to help the lawyers reach the right decision for their careers. Sometimes, that means staying in their current firm.

This, however, is very different from the lateral who stays in his current firm out of inertia, fear of change, or an unwillingness to get out of his comfort zone. Lawyers who remain with the status quo for these reasons are committing one of the biggest career mistakes we see.

Opportunities only come around so many times in someone's career. Years of experience, client base, expertise, and reputation are all essential components of a career, and of course they are constantly changing. At certain points in your career, these components occasionally will line up such that you have a compelling opportunity to take your career to the next level. These types of opportunities are rare. Even for laterals who are coveted in the market—those with large books of business and good rates—certain unique opportunities will only present themselves once in a lawyer's career.

If you have a genuinely good reason to turn down such an opportunity, then that must be respected. But if the decision to turn down an opportunity is not based on a genuinely good reason, then you are making a major career mistake.

By the way, "the timing is not right" is rarely a good reason to turn down a transformational offer. The timing is never right for a major career change. It will never be a perfect time for a lateral move.

If timing is a real issue, the hiring firm can usually work it out with you. For example, if you want to move to Firm A, but you are expecting a major bonus or distribution in four months, then that of course is a valid issue. But rather than turning down a great offer for that reason, you would be much wiser to discuss the issue with Firm A. Firm A is probably very willing to work out a resolution that is attractive to you.

Firm A could offer to pay the amount of the expected bonus or distribution. Or Firm A could work out an agreement on compensation, title, and everything else with you, but with the further agreement that you will not be joining Firm A for another four months or until you collect the bonus or distribution. Rather than turning down a great situation because of "timing," you are much better off discussing the timing issue and working out a mutually satisfactory arrangement.

3. JUMPING TOO OFTEN

Yes, I know—I have been advocating for lateral moves. Yet while it is a critical career mistake to stay with the status quo because of inertia or a fear of change, it can be an equally big career mistake to move too often.

Even in the 21st century when lawyers are expected to practice with a number of firms throughout their careers, it is possible to make too many moves in too short of a time period. When this happens, it sends up red flags to other potential law firms that might otherwise be an ideal fit. There is still a stigma to being seen as a "job hopper."

So how long should you stay in a job before it is appropriate to move? The rule of thumb for professional employment has always been to stay in any job a minimum of one year. But for partner-level attorneys, that rule of thumb is more like three years, absent some truly compelling reasons to the contrary.

This is because, in general, it takes a lateral at least a year or two to become fully integrated into a new firm. Aside from the day-to-day matters, such as learning the best lunch spots and the names of the other lawyers and staff on your floor, it takes time to transition the major clients, learn new timekeeping and billing systems, and figure out which lawyers are good options for various types of cross-selling and spin-off work—both work coming from you and coming to you.

Of course, there are exceptions, and when a great opportunity arises, the wise lawyer learns about it, at a minimum. Otherwise, three years is a good rule of thumb for partner-level lawyers.

The best way to avoid the "job hopper" label is, of course, to engage in fewer lateral moves. Try to follow the three-year rule *and* only make a lateral move that is clearly a step up in compensation, prestige, and/or practice (e.g., rates, sophistication, clients).

4. THE PITFALLS OF GOING IN-HOUSE

Every lawyer who has ever been in private practice has thought about going in-house. No more time sheets. No more pressure to bill more hours. No more pressure to bring in business. Supervising outside counsel, as opposed to being supervised outside counsel. Having only one client, and really getting to know that client like the back of your hand. Becoming General Counsel and leading a legal department. The possibility of moving into the C Suite, and perhaps even becoming the CEO one day. The appeal of going in-house is obvious.

For some lawyers, going in-house is the best possible career move. These lawyers make the move and never look back. Many of them spend the rest of their careers as in-house counsel for the same company. Others make "lateral moves" between different corporate legal departments and climb that career ladder, and it works out very well for them.

There are major pitfalls to going in-house, however, that you should consider.

For starters, partner-level lawyers who go in-house are giving up a tremendous amount of autonomy and independence. In a law firm, you are the economic engine of the entity. You are the revenue generator, whether you bring it in the door, perform the actual work, or both. You are the most important person in a law firm, by far. You are the reason law firms exist.

Few people in our society have more independence and career autonomy than a lawyer in private practice with her own client base. If you are in private practice and have enough business to be self-sufficient (meaning you do not need to be given work by anyone else in order to stay busy full-time and/ or you originate enough business to cover your compensation and your share of firm overhead, at a minimum), then you can literally make your own path. If your current firm is taking good care of you by way of compensation, resources, culture, and prestige, then you probably will decide to remain.

If one of these elements changes to your dissatisfaction, or if you believe there is a better opportunity elsewhere, you have the option to leave. Generally speaking, you can move your practice to any number of firms that are more to your liking. Stated differently, you can take your ball and go home.

This is a tremendous advantage for lawyers in private practice. They are extremely mobile and, barring something unusual, are able to work almost anywhere they want. These lawyers are not stuck. If they have enough business, they are *always* in demand in the private practice sector.

In-house lawyers, on the other hand, are not in such an enviable position. Yes, they can move to other in-house positions, and they often do, but not at will. There have to be openings in other in-house legal departments, and those openings have to match the background of the lawyer who wants to move. If there are none that match the lawyer's experience and background, then the in-house lawyer is stuck. Depending on his area of expertise and geographic restrictions for family or other reasons, he may be stuck for a long time.

Additionally, while important, respected, and well paid, in-house lawyers are not the economic engines of companies, nor are they the *most* important persons in the organization. At the end of the day, they are not the reason the company exists, but an expense item on the P&L. This is obviously very different from how lawyers in law firms are considered.

Certain events can create even worse pitfalls for in-house lawyers. I have seen them happen too many times. Every day, companies are sold. They are acquired. They merge with other companies. They go bankrupt. They restructure their legal departments. Every time one of these events occurs, the in-house lawyers at these companies are impacted in a major, sometimes life-altering way. These events inevitably result in some, or all, of the lawyers in an in-house department losing their jobs.

When this happens, of course the ideal scenario is that all of the affected lawyers are able to find new positions in their current markets. But realistically, that will not happen for some of them. Again, there must be other in-house openings, and those openings must match the expertise and experience level of each of the affected lawyers for this ideal scenario to happen. That is highly unlikely.

Another option for the affected lawyer is to move to a new city where she can find an in-house position that matches her expertise and experience level. This happens frequently, and people relocate to new cities every day, but few would argue it is an easy process, especially when it impacts other people such as family members.

The final option for the affected lawyer is to return to private practice. This also happens every day, and sometimes very successfully. Most of the time, however, the affected lawyer is forced to accept substantially lower compensation than her experience level would warrant because she has no business to bring with her.

Coming from in-house, most lawyers who return to private practice do not have a book of business. There are always exceptions to this, and some lawyers are able to return to private practice with business from their previous company or its successor. However, this is relatively rare. With no book of business, compensation will be significantly less than that of her peer who is at the same level of experience, but who has remained in private practice and generates significant originations for the law firm.

5. POORLY CHOSEN PRACTICE AREA SELECTION

Practice area selection is perhaps the most poorly executed aspect of becoming a lawyer. There are literally hundreds of ways in which a lawyer can use his law degree, and the day-to-day activities among them vary widely. Extroverts, introverts, research specialists, government gurus, numbers lovers, writers, speakers, and many other types of people can find a legal practice area that fits them well.

The problem is the legal industry, including law schools, has not developed a good system for helping law school students and graduates determine which practice areas are the right fit for them, and which are not. Consequently, many lawyers end up practicing in areas for which they are a poor fit and are relatively unhappy in their careers.

Law students may be fortunate enough to have some real-life exposure. There are internships and externships, summer clerk opportunities, and even work in legal clinics for some fortunate students. But not all students have these opportunities, and even for those who do, these only scratch the surface as far as exposing them to the options they have with their law degree.

Most law students either have no idea what type of law they want to practice, or they think they know what practice area they want based on a hunch or an article they read, or because they know someone who practices in that area, or they have a good professor who teaches in that area, or, frequently, because they were offered a job in that area. As a result, mismatched careers are common in the legal industry.

If you are a law student, or even a lawyer who is considering which practice area to pursue, you should research the various practice areas thoroughly. Talk to Career Services at your law school. Speak to lawyers who practice in the areas of potential interest. Try to learn what "a day in the life" is like. This may sound like a lot of effort, but if it can help you avoid choosing the wrong practice area, the effort will be more than worthwhile.

As you look into practice area selection, also understand that some practice areas typically have different bill rates and, consequently, pay differently than others. One prominent example is Employment law. This is a practice area found in most prestigious law firms, much like Commercial Real Estate, Corporate/Mergers and Acquisitions, Healthcare, and Commercial Litigation. Unlike those other practice areas, however, the billing rates for many Employment law matters have been significantly reduced in recent decades.

The reason for this broad reduction in rates is simple: insurance providers began offering coverage for Employment law matters. Employment Practices Liability Insurance (EPLI) covers businesses against claims by workers that their legal rights as employees of the company have been violated. These types of claims are typically not covered by other types of standard business insurance, such as E&O, D&O and General Liability Insurance. When the insurers began to offer EPLI coverage to more and more businesses, rates for Employment lawyers were pushed down because insurance coverage invariably drives down billing rates for lawyers.

This, of course, does not change the fundamentals of practicing Employment law. Lawyers who practice in this area find it extremely interesting and a rewarding way to help their business clients. To be sure, there are many Employment lawyers who do very well financially. As with all practice areas, however, lawyers who are considering Employment law as their practice focus should have a clear understanding of the rate issue, especially compared to other practice areas that typically serve business clients.

6. NOT SPENDING ENOUGH TIME ON BUSINESS DEVELOPMENT

Of all the career mistakes I see younger lawyers make, the most common one is not spending enough time on business development. This is understandable, particularly for hardworking associates who are expected (required) to bill a high number of hours each year. There are only so many hours in the day. By the time a lawyer has billed eight-plus hours in a given day, that leaves very little time for cultivating clients and developing business, especially if the lawyer wants to have any semblance of a family life or personal life.

Nevertheless, any lawyer in private practice must spend a sufficient amount of time on business development if she hopes to make partner and have a successful career. Too many young lawyers make the mistake of thinking that if they just bill enough hours and generate enough revenue through their personal production, then that will be enough. They fall into the trap of thinking they can worry about bringing in clients later, when they are more experienced and more established. This can be a major career misstep.

Business development is absolutely vital if you are in private practice and want to achieve significant career success. Again, I have told countless young attorneys that if they have one hour to spend before they leave work on a given day, they should spend that hour on marketing and business development as opposed to billing. Obviously, this assumes no pressing deadlines. On a typical, normal workday, an hour spent on client development is simply more important in the long run than billing another hour.

Some firms may take issue with this statement, but again, think about this: when a downturn happens, and law firms begin to lay off attorneys or de-equitize them or reduce their points, which lawyers are on the receiving end of these unpleasant but necessary measures? Is it the rainmakers? Or is it the service partners? Is it the lawyers who bring in the business and are considered the most valuable lawyers within the firm? Or is it the lawyers who do the work, the very important but not indispensable grinders? The answer should serve as your guide if you want to make it to the top of the law firm ladder.

7. CHOOSING A CULTURE THAT DOES NOT FIT

It is a truism that law firms all have different cultures. Yes, some are quite similar, but there are always differences, sometimes significant ones. Genuine career success requires you to select a firm that is the right cultural fit. Sometimes lawyers do not realize their firm is a poor cultural fit at first, especially those who joined their current firms when they were younger. If you realize your current firm is not a good cultural match, you should seriously consider a lateral move to a firm that is a better match if you want to have a thriving practice.

Cultural fit is not solely referring to personalities, dress code, and how the lawyers interact with each other and staff, although those are certainly a part of it. Cultural fit for law firms also relates to how the firm practices, what the rate structure is, the work ethic, the compensation system, firm leadership, and similar factors that directly impact the lawyer's practice and income.

To take a simplistic example, the lawyer who is a great rainmaker wants to make sure her firm rewards originations. The grinder wants a heavier emphasis on personal production (i.e., working attorney) revenues. The lawyer who likes to work as part of a team needs to be with a firm that emphasizes collaboration and teamwork. Meanwhile, the lawyer who loves business development, but needs sufficient resources, wants to make sure he is in a firm that has a similar view of supporting (i.e., investing in) business development efforts.

Lawyers who are practicing in a firm that is a poor cultural fit have usually made one of two mistakes. The first mistake is joining a firm as a lateral without doing sufficient due diligence on the firm's culture. This one happens more than it should. The second occurs when a lawyer realizes his current firm is a bad cultural fit, but he is unwilling to make a change anyway, whether it is because of inertia, fear of change, or a misplaced sense of loyalty. These same lawyers would see their practices (and often their incomes) soar in a different law firm culture.

In sum, once you realize your current firm is a bad cultural fit, start looking. Once you find a firm that you believe is a good cultural fit, conduct proper due diligence.

8. CHOOSING THE WRONG CITY

This is certainly not an issue unique to the legal industry, but if you are a law student or newer lawyer making a career decision, you must consider geographic market realities as a critical factor in your process.

For some, this is not even an issue. Some are able and willing to go wherever the best market is for their practice area, whether that is a major market like New York or Los Angeles, an international destination on the other side of the world, or a small town where they can be the dominant lawyer in the area.

For others, their job is not the only consideration. Spouses, life partners, parents, children, and even siblings and friends in some instances factor significantly into selecting a city. Many lawyers simply are not able to move to any market in the country (or the world). This, of course, is not a career mistake, although it can have a major impact on their careers.

The mistake we see is when a lawyer chooses a practice area that is simply incompatible with his geographic market. Often this happens as a result of a relocation. Let's say you have established a practice area in a certain market. Then because of a spouse or life partner's job, or because of family obligations or some other reason, you relocate to a different city where your practice area is simply not compatible.

Sometimes these lawyers try to continue their practice in their new market. Certainly, with remote work becoming more common and constantly improving technology, some lawyers are able to continue with their practice from a different geographic market. For others, however, this is often trying to fit a square peg into a round hole. These lawyers end up frustrated because they insist on working in their former practice area in their new geographic market, and it just does not work.

For example, if you want to work on the biggest, most sophisticated international transactions, you are not going to find that work in a mid-tier city. A Public Finance lawyer is going to need to be in a metropolitan area with enough projects to sustain a viable practice. Entertainment lawyers are going to find much more work in cities such as Los Angeles and Nashville than they are in other markets. Equine lawyers may be able to build a successful practice in Kentucky, but not in most other states.

If it is not feasible to generate enough remote work in your chosen practice area, and you are stuck in an incompatible location, your best option is to select a new practice area. This is not ideal, and no one likes to begin anew, but the alternative is ongoing frustration. Many lawyers cannot change the realities of their new geographic market. However, they can change their practice area focus.

9. SACRIFICING PHYSICAL AND MENTAL HEALTH

Everyone in the legal industry understands sacrifice. It is impossible to graduate from law school and have a successful law practice without making enormous personal sacrifices. The demands of the profession are simply too great.

There is a difference, however, between making necessary personal sacrifices and sacrificing one's physical and mental health. The former is unavoidable and is the cost of participation in the industry. The latter is a major mistake that not only can damage one's career but also can literally destroy lives.

Extremely long hours; deadlines; pressures from clients, courts, and supervising attorneys; academic pressures for law students; and other sources of stress are part of the equation for practicing law. But when these stressors cause lawyers to ignore their physical health, such as by not exercising or rarely going outside, or primarily eating fast food and takeout, it will inevitably cause damage. Without good physical health, it will be difficult for any lawyer to maintain a successful law practice.

The same applies when it comes to mental health. Lawyers have higher rates of depression and suicide than many professions in our society. It is common knowledge that mental health problems affect attorneys at a higher rate than most professions in the United States. Moreover, substance abuse is rampant in the legal world. Whether it is with alcohol or drugs or both, lawyers are more prone than most to self-medicate with these substances.

Another dangerous practice that affects mental health as well as physical health is excessively sacrificing family, friends, and all personal time. Again, some sacrifice cannot be avoided. But when lawyers become so wrapped up in their work and the stressors that go along with it that they rarely see their family and friends, and literally have no life outside of work, that is a major problem. That is not healthy. They start to lose perspective, and, ironically, it eventually diminishes their effectiveness as lawyers.

Every lawyer, whether she is early in her career or a seasoned veteran, needs to take the time to care for herself both physically and mentally. It is almost impossible to achieve long-term career success without doing so.

10. EXPECTING A LARGE INCREASE IN COMPENSATION

One mistake we see with regularity is laterals expecting to receive a large increase in guaranteed compensation as a part of their recruitment. In a way, this expectation makes sense. After all, most laterals (by definition) are practicing at a good firm and have established successful careers. If they are going to make a move to a different firm, then that different firm needs to be prepared to pay for it.

To an extent, this is often what happens. As noted throughout this book, law firms have to pay in order to attract the best and brightest. Lawyers usually are not looking to take a pay cut.

However, there is a big difference between laterals not wanting to take a pay cut and laterals expecting a major increase in guaranteed pay as a requirement for making a lateral move. The first is perfectly reasonable. The latter usually will not happen, absent a truly unusual and compelling reason.

Law firms have gotten smarter about lateral hiring. Very few firms are still willing to "buy lawyers" on a regular basis. Are there exceptions? Do law firms pay over and above for superstars? Absolutely, yes. But we are talking about the norm, and law firms are no longer going to pay excessive amounts guaranteed for multiple years for lateral talent. The lessons learned from the past have made law firms much more reluctant to offer extremely lucrative, long-term guaranteed deals to lateral attorneys.

This means prospective laterals need to understand market realities. Unless they are true superstars, they usually are not going to be paid well above market value to make a lateral move. They might have the *opportunity* to earn a significant increase in compensation based on performance, and they should have that opportunity as part of making the lateral move. However, if their only interest in considering a lateral move is for a short-term, guaranteed, major increase in pay, then they are making a mistake and wasting everyone's time.

A lateral move is a long-term play, and it is a mistake to view it otherwise.

11. NOT LEVERAGING THEIR POWER

This is a career mistake made by more experienced lawyers, as opposed to younger ones. Some may not even view this as a mistake. It is an old-school perspective, and some lawyers view it as essential to maintaining collegiality and harmonious relations among partners. I am referring to the situations in which some lawyers consistently leave money on the table for "the good of the firm."

In a way, it is admirable. It is generous, and it certainly can improve relations among partners. In our view, however, if it happens over the course of three to five or more years, it is a career mistake.

Certainly, lawyers within a firm should help each other and look out for each other. Certainly, every lawyer will have bad years due to market conditions, personal matters, or other legitimate reasons, and well-run law firms take these factors into account when allocating points, distributions, and bonuses.

Nevertheless, we believe it is a mistake, and ultimately self-defeating, for a highly productive lawyer to not fully capitalize on his efforts and success year after year. First, it discourages very high performance from other lawyers within the firm, which hurts the organization and, ultimately, the lawyers in it. Moreover, it is simply unfair to the highest-producing lawyers. If your performance consistently is worth $1 million on the open market and you consistently accept $800,000 from your current firm in order to maintain firm harmony or because of internal partner compensation ratios, you would be making a career mistake.

12. NOT PREPARING CLIENTS FOR YOUR LATERAL MOVE

From the viewpoint of the hiring law firm, one of the worst things that can happen with a lateral attorney is when he does not bring his clients with him when he joins their firm. Or, more commonly, he brings some but not most of his clients when he joins their firm. This is probably the biggest complaint when it comes to lateral hiring. Almost every firm in America has experienced some version of this scenario: "he said he was going to bring all of this business, and he actually brought less than half of that."

As we all know, this is the client's prerogative. The client, and only the client, gets to decide which lawyer(s) she is going to use. If the client decides not to follow an attorney to his new law firm, then that is well within her discretion to decide.

What we consider a career mistake is when the client makes this decision because she was not prepared by her lawyer for the impending move. She was caught off guard, and most people in business do not like to be surprised.

As we discussed in Chapters 8 and 9, this is a delicate situation. The lateral cannot inform his clients of his departure before he has given notice to his partners. This is a fiduciary duty the lateral owes to his current partners, and of course he cannot breach this duty.

However, there is a wide gap between breaching the fiduciary duty you owe your current partners and allowing your client to be completely surprised by the announcement of your lateral departure. There is ample room between these two poles in which you, a thoughtful lawyer, can make sure you do not violate your fiduciary duties *and* make sure your client is not caught off guard by your lateral departure.

13. FORGETTING THAT THE LATERAL IS A SELLER AS WELL AS A BUYER

In the previous chapter, we discussed how one of the major mistakes a law firm can make in the lateral hiring process is forgetting the lateral must be recruited. Laterals are not applying for a job. Firms that want to hire good laterals need to recruit them and should understand the lateral probably has a number of options, including the option to remain where she is.

Nevertheless, as a lateral, you would be making a similar mistake if you act as though you call all of the shots, because you do not. Any good firm is going to evaluate a prospective lateral in a number of different ways. Certainly, your practice economics is one of the most important considerations for any law firm that is pursuing lateral talent.

Of equal importance to wise law firms is cultural fit, which includes the ability to get along well with others. Some lawyers tend to overlook this consideration and make the mistake of thinking this is less important than their numbers. Indeed, for some firms, the numbers will rule regardless. But in other firms, cultural fit is given almost equal weight compared to the numbers. I have seen many highly profitable lawyers rejected by good law firms because of how they conducted themselves.

Arrogance, condescension, and haughtiness are not attractive to anyone, including law firms. Prospective laterals sometimes display these attributes because they are in high demand, and they know it. Everyone wants them (or at least it seems that way to them). Everyone is wooing them. It is easy to get caught up in this and forget that they also need to be selling themselves.

It is true they are not "looking for a job," and the law firm in question should be selling themselves too. Presumably, though, the law firm has many strong selling points and is not desperate to hire. The firm will not collapse if it does not hire the lateral.

If you are interested in a firm, then you need to sell yourself just as much as the firm needs to sell itself.

14. NOT HAVING A COMPELLING REASON

Being in the legal search business, I am certainly in favor of lawyers exploring other career options. No surprise there. When these other options create opportunities for lawyers to improve their practices and increase their compensation, then I absolutely encourage lawyers to pursue them. However, I also firmly believe lawyers need to have a compelling reason before making a lateral move.

The career mistake made by some lawyers is making a lateral move for no particular reason. These lawyers have a vague hope that things will be different at a new firm, or they believe they need to change firms because they have been at Firm A for a number of years, and thus it is time to move to Firm B. These are not good reasons to make a lateral move.

The best reasons to make a lateral move are the ones we listed in Chapter 6. Usually, these will in some way improve your practice, increase your opportunities to bring in more business, and, ultimately, produce more income for you.

It is true that occasionally, lawyers can grow stale at a firm. When lawyers believe they have grown stale at their current firm, my first piece of advice to them is to take a step back and evaluate their particular situation. If taking a step back entails taking some time off, and taking time off is feasible, then all the better. Sometimes a few days or weeks off is all that is needed. Sometimes lawyers have not grown stale as much as simply needing to recharge their batteries.

If, after taking time to reflect and evaluate, and ideally after taking some time off, you still believe you have grown stale at your current firm, then exploring lateral opportunities makes good sense. A fresh start can do wonders for people, and lawyers are no exception.

When this happens, a fresh start *is* the compelling reason for pursuing a lateral move. This is very different, though, from making a lateral move for no reason. A fresh start is a perfectly valid reason, but only after you have taken the time to properly evaluate your situation.

15. UNDERSELLING YOURSELF AND YOUR BOOK

Certainly, overselling (i.e., overpromising) is a major career mistake for any lateral. And yes, there are some lawyers out there who make claims regarding their practice, particularly their client base, that are inaccurate if not outright false. Such an approach is harmful to the hiring firm, of course, but also quite harmful to the lateral. The lateral may have set himself up with a large salary for a period of time, but it will not last long if the law firm was wise enough to avoid a long-term, guaranteed compensation agreement.

Eventually, an attorney's performance will speak for itself. If a firm hires a lawyer because he has convinced them that he is bringing a large book of business with him, ultimately the truth will prevail. The lateral will either generate the amount of business he claims to have, or he will not. If his actual book of business is substantially below what he claimed he would bring with him, then the hiring firm will either terminate him or greatly reduce his compensation.

In other words, it is clearly a career mistake for a lawyer to overpromise the size of his book, but it is not a mistake that endures. The lawyer's performance will speak for itself in due time, and adjustments will be made if necessary.

The more common mistake, lawyers underselling their practice and book of business, can be equally harmful to the lawyer because it is longer term. It may not be as harmful to the hiring firm, but it still deprives them of the opportunity to make an accurate evaluation of needed legal talent.

Contrary to popular belief, I have found that lateral attorneys are much more likely to undersell themselves and their books of business than to oversell. There are several reasons for this. First, as we all know, there are no guarantees with clients and their business. In theory, every client in America could fire every one of their attorneys today. Of course, that is highly unlikely, but in theory it is possible. No lawyer can *guarantee* any client or any amount of business will port with her. And both lawyers and law firms alike prefer guarantees, not surprises. Unfortunately, absolute certainty is not an option in lateral hiring and determining portable business. The best lawyers can do is make good faith, informed estimates.

Another reason laterals sometimes underestimate their

books is because they do not want to put a target on their backs. This is understandable. Lawyers who claim to have a significant book of business usually also receive significant compensation packages. When a lawyer is new to a firm and commanding a large salary, especially when compared to lawyers who have been with the hiring firm for a long time, she is going to get a lot of attention. Every month or quarter, or whenever the partners receive firm financials and performance reports, they will be looking closely to see whether she deserves (in their opinion) the large amount of money the firm is paying out to her. Some lawyers would rather underestimate their book of business and take less money from the outset, and then later catch up on compensation in the form of bonuses for performance. There is much less attention paid to them in this manner, and they are betting on themselves to perform.

The third reason lawyers sometimes undersell themselves and their book of business is related to the second: some lawyers have a strong personal belief in underpromising and overdelivering. This is often a personality trait, and for these lawyers, this trait is often not only reserved for professional situations. As a general rule of living, they believe the best approach is to set expectations lower and let their strong performance be a pleasant surprise. I have known lawyers who, when asked to estimate their book of business, would take their true originations for the past three to five years and then cut that in half as their estimate. If such a lawyer had a legitimate $1.5 million book, he would project it as $750,000 to a prospective hiring firm.

All these reasons are understandable. It is hard to blame someone for wanting certainty, wanting to avoid excessive scrutiny, or preferring to undersell and overdeliver instead of the opposite. Regardless of the validity of reasons, however, underselling is a mistake.

When lawyers undersell themselves and their book, they can deprive themselves of fantastic, career-changing opportunities. I have seen lawyers who undersold themselves and, in doing so, did not receive offers that they absolutely deserved and would have received with a more accurate projection of their practice and book. I have seen other lawyers who received offers, but these offers were much lower than they would have been with accurate projections. In addition to causing lawyers to miss out on great offers and more money, underselling can cost them in firm resources, reputation, and standing within the hiring firm.

The last reason it is a mistake to intentionally undersell is because it is not true. Law firms, just like any business, rely on accurate financial projections to make decisions. Inaccurate projections, even when they are pleasant surprises, are less beneficial to the firm than accurate ones.

16. NOT HAVING A BUSINESS PLAN

All lawyers need a business plan, whether they are considering a lateral move or not. Moreover, a lawyer's business plan should be updated annually and reviewed at least quarterly. It should be considered a living document that changes as the lawyer's practice and situation changes through the years.

Unfortunately, few attorneys have a business plan at all, let alone have one they revise every year and review every quarter. One of the reasons so few lawyers have business plans is because creating a business plan seems like a daunting task to a busy lawyer. Creating a 20-plus page document seems like an inefficient use of time to lawyers who mainly bill by the hour.

Fortunately, your business plan does not have to be overly complicated, and it certainly does not have to be 20-plus pages. Your business plan is really an outline of your practice and where you want to take it. Although there are numerous formats that you can use, a solid business plan should contain the following:

- Statement of your current practice. This includes practice area details, clients, and revenues.
- Declaration of where you would like to be. What do you envision for yourself and your practice in the next two, four, eight years, and beyond?
- Explanation of how you will achieve the goals declared for the next two, four, eight years, and beyond. This is the strategy component of the plan. How will you grow your practice? What is the specific approach that will enable you to hit the origination goals? What contacts will you leverage? What expertise do you have, or will you have, that will help execute the strategy?

For prospective laterals, it is essential to include in the strategy explanation a detailed analysis of how you will leverage the hiring firm's resources to achieve your goals. In other words, you should explain that because the hiring firm has X, Y, and Z, you will be able to use X, Y, and Z to increase your business so that your goals (as declared in the plan) will be attained. This explanation should be logical and realistic. Without criticizing, you should also explain any limitations found in your current firm that are not found in the hiring firm, such as geographic limitations, lack of bench strength, and insufficient practice area expertise.

A solid attorney business plan is an essential document for all lawyers. If you are exploring a lateral move, having one can make the difference between receiving your dream offer or not.

17. INSUFFICIENT DUE DILIGENCE

Conducting due diligence is such a critical part of the lateral hiring process that we have devoted an entire chapter to it. Please see Chapter 10 for an in-depth analysis.

V

Special Considerations in Lateral Hiring

CHAPTER 13

OLDER LAWYERS: HOW TO WIN THE FOURTH QUARTER

OVER THE YEARS, I HAVE OBSERVED AN INTERESTING phenomenon with lawyers in their upper 50s and older. Depending on their exact age, personal desires, and individual situations, these lawyers generally have between five and 20 years left of active, full-time work. A significant number of these lawyers have a sincere interest in doing "something different" with the rest of their careers. For many of them, doing something different entails some type of lateral move. Because they are in a later stage of their careers, these lateral moves are often different from the ones we have been discussing in this book.

Nearly all of these lawyers have been successful. Many of them have earned and saved enough money so that compensation is much less important than it used to be. They universally tell me they could remain in their current position with their current firm, and that would be fine. They can continue with what they are doing, keep earning top compensation, and stay on the same path until retirement. And many of them do just that.

Some of them, however, are so driven by the excitement of a new challenge that they make a bold move. They leave their current firm, where typically they have been practicing for many years, and move to a new place. This can look like any number of things. Sometimes, these moves look like other lateral moves. These lawyers decide to play out the fourth quarter of their careers in a different firm, for one or more of the reasons we have covered in this book.

However, sometimes their reason for making a move is one that is unique to lawyers in the fourth quarter of their careers. Among these lawyers, I have seen them choose one of the following paths:

1. GOING IN-HOUSE

Yes, almost all lawyers in private practice have at least some level of interest in going in-house. Frequently, this is not feasible for lawyers in the prime of their careers because of financial reasons. While there are certainly exceptions, generally speaking, successful lawyers in private practice with their own clients make more money than in-house lawyers. Though many would love to be rid of time sheets and the never-ending quest for more clients, they simply cannot take the reduction in compensation at that stage in their lives.

Once those lawyers are in their upper 50s and 60s, however, a reduction in pay is often less of a deterrent. They have always wanted to experience life as an in-house lawyer, and this is the time to do it.

2. STARTING A NEW OFFICE

Some lawyers are very attracted to the challenge of starting a brand-new office. They love the idea of building something. They like the entrepreneurial excitement of creating something from nothing. They want to lead a team and spend the fourth quarter of their practice establishing and growing a brand-new office. This usually does not mean starting a new law firm, although occasionally it does. More often, this means starting the new office of an existing firm. In other words, it is usually a law firm expansion.

Some lawyers are fortunate enough to get this opportunity, especially if they live and practice in a city with a thriving legal market. In hot legal markets, out-of-town law firms are constantly trying to establish a new presence there. Ideally, these firms will acquire a smaller firm or practice group and plant their flag with these newly hired/acquired lawyers. However, many will start much smaller, whether by design or necessity. These law firms will start with one or two lawyers who will lateral to the firm for the purpose of establishing the firm's office in this new city. Often, these laterals are lawyers in the fourth quarter of their practice who have embraced the exciting challenge of starting and building a new office.

To be clear, some lawyers have absolutely no interest in building anything other than their own practice. The thought of building an office from scratch sounds exhausting to them, rather than exciting. But for a certain type of lawyer, establishing and growing a brand-new office can be a very rewarding way to conclude a successful career.

3. JOINING A DIFFERENT TYPE OF FIRM

There are more ways to practice law today than there have ever been. There are, of course, many different types of traditional law firms, ranging from giant Am Law 50 firms with lawyers and offices all around the world to sole practitioners who work out of their homes. In between, there are regional firms, super-regional firms, national firms, local firms, small firms, midsize firms, and boutiques. Additionally, there are a growing number of truly different firms with different models.

One type of firm that is growing in popularity is the virtual law firm, or distributed law firm as it is sometimes called. These firms typically employ lawyers across the country or across a specific region in most of the same practice areas found in traditional large law firms. However, the lawyers in these firms usually work from home or from a small, modest workspace that may or may not be paid for by the firm. In addition to minimal, usually modest office space, these types of firms also hold staff size to a minimum and eliminate as many other bells and whistles as possible.

As a result, the overhead for these law firms can be a fraction of the overhead incurred by most traditional law firms. The low overhead results in lower billing rates, which obviously appeals to clients and creates significant business development oppor-tunities. This often results in higher incomes for the lawyers who practice in these firms.

Furthermore, these firms often utilize a formulaic com-pensation model, which means the lawyers know exactly how much money they will make. These lawyers enjoy the control they have over their own practices and their own income. They are not dependent on someone else's decisions or production for their personal income. Although there are drawbacks to virtual or distributed firms, such as reduced camaraderie and in-person collaboration, there are clearly a number of benefits that make these firms a good fit for some lawyers, including some lawyers in the fourth quarter of their careers.

In addition to virtual or distributed firms, there are a variety of other law firm models that utilize a purely formulaic compensation model. Some traditional law firms have adopted this model while retaining all of the other customary components of a large traditional firm.

Some law firms have adopted a unique governance model, of which a purely formulaic compensation system is an essential part. For these firms, law firm ownership is usually controlled by one person or a small handful of people who run the firm and handle the administrative duties of the firm. The lawyers there contribute either a set dollar amount or a set percentage to cover overhead and then keep the rest of the revenue for themselves.

Still other law firm models do not even require their attorneys to have any business. For these entities, there are individuals who are responsible for bringing in clients, and the lawyers only have to perform legal work. Others within the entity handle business development, administrative duties, and everything else.

For lawyers who are in the fourth quarter and who are seeking something different, some of these models can be very appealing. Sometimes lawyers want to just practice law and take care of their clients. They do not want to worry about governance issues or red tape. Sometimes, the lawyers do not even want to worry about getting and/or keeping clients. They literally just want to practice law as they finish out their careers. These various types of law firm models and compensation models can be a great option for some lawyers.

4. CHANGING PRACTICE AREAS

Some lawyers play out the fourth quarter of their careers by making a move many lawyers dream about—they change practice areas, the most frequent of which is moving to a plaintiff's firm. Most defense litigators have at least thought about life on the other side. They think about life without time sheets, clients who are more grateful than demanding, and, of course, those multimillion-dollar verdicts and settlements.

One reason more of them do not make the move is because of the risk involved. Being a plaintiff's lawyer with a contingency fee model can certainly be lucrative, but it can be very risky. These risks can lead to significant financial stress. For many defense litigators who are making a very comfortable living at a minimum, the risk is simply too much.

This risk tolerance sometimes changes as these lawyers reach the fourth quarter, however. Some defense lawyers who have put their kids through college, built up equity in their homes, and padded their retirement accounts are in a different financial situation than they were in earlier in their careers. Additionally, they have 30-plus years of litigation experience under their belt and are confident in their abilities. A number of these lawyers finish their careers litigating for the other side.

5. WORKING OUTSIDE OF THE LAW

Almost every lawyer has, at some point in her career, thought about leaving the law entirely. Although the law can be a rewarding, intellectually challenging, and financially lucrative career field, it has its drawbacks, as every career field does. Lawyers are usually intelligent, ambitious, and driven people, and it is natural for lawyers to wonder whether their noteworthy skills could be utilized in careers outside of law.

The main reason most lawyers never leave the law, even those who would like to do so, is because the law usually pays them substantially more than they could make outside of the law, at least initially. The law can and often does put "golden handcuffs" on lawyers, which makes it all but impossible for many of them to leave the field.

By the fourth quarter, though, those golden handcuffs are less restrictive for some lawyers. As we have covered, lawyers 55 and up are often in a much different financial situation than they were earlier in their careers. They can afford to take more risks, and for a small minority of lawyers, this entails leaving the law altogether.

The careers pursued by these former lawyers are as varied as one might imagine. Entire books have been written on this very topic. Among the many career fields pursued by former lawyers are writers, teachers, consultants, entrepreneurs, financial advisors, and investment bankers—and those are only a fraction.

CHAPTER 14

LATERAL HIRING IN SMALLER FIRMS

AS EVERY LAWYER WHO HAS PRACTICED IN ONE CAN TELL you, small firms have both advantages and disadvantages when compared to larger law firms. If you are a leader of a small firm looking to hire laterals, this chapter is for you. We will cover the unique pros and cons that both you and your prospective laterals should be considering.

First, let's examine exactly what we mean when we use the term "small firm." Certainly, it depends on the geographic area. A small firm in New York City might be considered a large firm in Wyoming. Also, a small office is not the same as a small firm. Even very large firms often have a few offices that contain only a small number of lawyers. Nevertheless, the lawyers in these small offices enjoy many of the same resources and depth of expertise, as well as the inherent challenges, as the other lawyers who practice in the bigger offices of that same large firm.

Although there are no binding definitions and it certainly varies by market, generally speaking, a large firm has over 100 lawyers. A midsize firm has 40–100 lawyers, and a small firm has fewer than 40 lawyers.

Why do some lawyers want to practice in a small firm? Isn't bigger always better? Actually, there are numerous reasons some lawyers prefer a small firm, and we will look at a few of the most common.

First, the culture of a small firm is easier to establish and maintain than a larger firm. It is much easier to get 20 or 30 lawyers to buy into doing things a certain way than it is with 200 or 300.

Also, and probably related, collegiality is generally better in smaller firms. To some extent, this is inevitable. A lawyer with 25 partners is going to have close relationships with a much higher percentage of her partners than a lawyer with 250 partners.

Finally, lawyers in smaller firms usually have a much greater voice in firm decisions than those in larger firms. If a law firm has 15 partners, each and every one of those partners has input and some degree of influence within the firm. At large firms, the majority of partners have almost zero input, other than the ability to vote.

Of course, there are disadvantages to practicing in a small firm as well. Smaller firms have, by definition, limited manpower. As a result, small firms are usually not asked to handle very large cases and transactions. General Counsel and CEOs typically view small firms as too risky to handle the largest legal matters, not because of skill level, but because of limited manpower.

In addition to this, small firms have fewer resources than large firms. They simply cannot put as much into their matters because they are entities with tens of millions of dollars in revenue, compared to large firms with hundreds of millions of dollars (or more) in revenue.

Similarly, small firms have limited services they can offer. Even in small firms that are "full service," they simply cannot provide the same level of expertise in as many different practice areas as large firms. The same applies to geographic footprint. These limitations invariably result in missed opportunities with clients who want their outside counsel to handle numerous legal issues in multiple jurisdictions.

When it comes to lateral hiring, some of the inherent advantages found in smaller firms can be very attractive to prospective laterals. Most lawyers would like to work in a firm with a positive culture. Collegiality is important to the vast majority of lawyers. After all, each of us spends the majority of our waking hours at work. It is much more appealing to spend those hours around people we like and support, and who like and support us. Most lawyers also like to have input on firm decisions. As highly intelligent, educated professionals, most lawyers want to have some say-so in the decisions that affect their work lives. Smaller firms can provide all of these benefits, and more, to prospective laterals.

On the other hand, thoughtful laterals are well aware of the potential drawbacks to joining a small firm, as noted above. These limitations can affect originations and billings, which, of course, affect income.

Another potential drawback for laterals is that small firms can be more vulnerable than large firms. A firm with 20–30 lawyers is almost certainly more dependent on fewer clients than a large firm. If one or two of the firm's key clients go away, because of acquisition or financial problems or they decide to no longer work with the small firm for whatever reason, the small firm could be in trouble.

Similarly, a small firm is much more dependent on its major rainmakers. If a firm has 20 lawyers, and five of them generate the majority of the business, what happens if two or three of them move laterally to another firm, become incapacitated, or die unexpectedly? The small firm can see a significant reduction in top-line revenue in these not uncommon scenarios. In a larger firm, these types of losses can be absorbed more easily because of numbers. If a firm has 50 elite rainmakers, losing two of them hurts much less than if a firm has five elite rainmakers and loses two of them.

When it comes to deciding between joining a large or a small firm, there is no universal right or wrong answer for the lateral who is fortunate enough to have options. However, it is critically important for this lateral to carefully weigh the pros and cons, and then make an informed decision as to which type of firm is best for her.

If you are a leader of a small firm and you would like to add lateral talent, your best path is to emphasize the inherent advantages your firm offers: culture, camaraderie, and input. Larger firms by their very nature simply cannot compete with you on these issues. For some lawyers, these issues are the most important ones and outweigh the advantages offered by larger firms, such as manpower, resources, practice area, and geographic coverage. To win the talent competition and grow your firm, your job is to find the prospective laterals who are seeking the advantages your firm can offer, and who are less interested in the others.

CHAPTER 15

GROUP HIRES AND LAW FIRM MERGERS

THIS CHAPTER DEALS WITH THE PROS AND CONS OF group hires and law firm mergers in more detail. Remember that these are just different types of lateral hiring. If you are the leader of a hiring firm considering these growth options, this chapter is for you.

GROUP HIRES

Even more than individual lateral hires, group hires are often the preferred growth strategy of law firms. When our legal search firm is engaged in lateral hiring projects for our clients, the majority of them will request group hires as an alternative, even a preferred alternative, to single lateral hires.

Of course, these group hires do not happen as often as single lateral hires. The transactions are more complicated because they involve more people and more clients. The more complicated a transaction, the less likely it is to occur. Nevertheless, most growing law firms have a definite desire for group hires.

The reasons for this desire are easy to understand. Group hires have several advantages over single lateral hires.

First, a group is going to have a greater impact than a single hire, even a high-profile single hire. The legal community notices group hires much more than single hires. This includes clients, lawyers in other firms, and the other lawyers in the hiring firm. It makes a bigger splash. This in turn helps attract clients and other prospective laterals.

Second, the financial effect is obviously much greater. A group of six lawyers, for example, is clearly going to produce more revenue than any single lateral. Economically, a group hire moves the needle more than a single hire.

Third, when an entire group makes a lateral move, the transition from the old firm to the new firm is often much smoother. Disagreements about clients, specific matters and files, compensation, work in progress, and the like are less likely to occur if there is no one left in that practice group at the former firm to fight for it. When an entire group moves, the former firm has a tendency to simply let them go without issues, provided everyone is acting reasonably. While this should happen also with single lateral moves, and it does much of the time, occasionally firms try to make things difficult for departing laterals, and it is easier to impose those difficulties on individuals than on groups.

Of course, there are some downsides to group hires. The main one is that hiring a group of lawyers is a much greater financial risk than hiring a single lateral. The firm is taking a bigger chance. A single lateral hire who does not work out is costly. A group hire that does not work out is exponentially more costly.

Another potential con for group hires has to do with integration and cultural fit. A single lateral is more likely to prioritize integration into the new firm and establishing relationships across the firm. Ideally, the lawyers within a group hire will do the same, and they often do. However, a group can unintentionally reduce the motivation to integrate and establish new relationships. The lawyers in a group have each other. If they are busy, and they probably will be, some members of the group will not make integration and new relationships a priority. This is not necessarily a disaster, but it can create strains and affect the firm's culture.

Lastly, group hires can create more conflicts than single lateral hires. Presumably, there are no deal-breaker conflicts from the outset because the hiring firm has already checked on that. However, conflicts will arise as rainmaker lawyers are out hustling for clients. Inevitably, this will lead to conflicts, and that usually means at least one lawyer is going to be displeased. If it happens too often, it can hurt the culture and lead to lateral departures.

In short, a group hire is a classic risk/reward strategy for the hiring firm. A successful group hire has a much greater impact on the hiring firm than a single successful lateral hire. An unsuccessful group hire has a much worse impact on the hiring firm than a single unsuccessful lateral hire.

LAW FIRM MERGERS

Law firm mergers are another high-risk/high-reward growth strategy often utilized by growing law firms. Mergers have many of the same pros and cons as group hires, except they are usually even more pronounced.

Unlike a group hire, a law firm merger involves absorbing

one entity into another. One firm, usually the smaller one, will no longer exist after the transaction is complete. This fact alone creates issues that are much more complex.

Additionally, law firm mergers usually involve more lawyers than a group hire, and more lawyers means more complications. Whereas group hires are typically between 3–20 lawyers, a law firm merger can involve hundreds of lawyers in the acquired firm. Of course, mergers of that size do not happen every day. Mergers involving 20–50+ lawyers in the acquired firm are more common.

Aside from compensation and the typical issues that arise in lateral hiring situations, law firm mergers create additional complexities. Even assuming the firms are on the same page with regard to culture, practice alignment, conflicts, bill rates, and compensation matters (and if they are not, then the firms should definitely rethink the merger), there are still numerous issues that must be negotiated and resolved. Among these issues are management structure, firm policies, technology and tele-communication, staff, capital contributions, assets of both firms, liabilities of both firms, office leases and real estate, and more.

For these reasons, law firm mergers, while certainly popular among some growing law firms, are not as common as group hires. Law firm mergers create the biggest impact, but they also have the most issues. Law firm leaders who pursue mergers as a growth strategy need to be mindful of these inherent issues and have a specific plan for overcoming the complexities that will inevitably arise.

CHAPTER 16

TALENT BROKERS

THERE ARE QUITE A FEW NAMES FOR WHAT MY COMPANY
does. Some of the most common ones are headhunter, recruiter,
and search consultant. The term I believe is most descriptive,
and the most accurate, is "talent broker." Similar to brokers
in other industries, those of us in the legal industry are in
the business of arranging transactions between a buyer and a
seller. In our world, the buyer is the law firm (or corporate legal
department) and the seller is the lateral candidate.

As brokers of legal talent, our job is to initiate communication between the law firm and the lateral candidate (in other
words, to make the introduction) and then to handle the details
of the transaction (the hiring process) all the way until the deal
is closed (the lateral is hired). Throughout this process, our job
is to make sure the transaction goes smoothly; to eliminate
as many obstacles as possible; to handle all of the necessary
details, such as LPQs, interviews, and salary negotiations; and,
ultimately, to close the deal.

Although most professionals have a basic understanding
of what talent brokers do, there is one widely held mispercep-

tion that should be corrected. A significant number of lawyers believe talent brokers work for the lawyers and are in the business of "finding people jobs." This is absolutely incorrect. Talent brokers are not in the business of finding people jobs. Talent brokers are in the business of filling needs for our clients, and our clients are the law firms and corporate legal departments that hire us and pay us.

Certainly, in the course of filling needs for our clients, we do in fact place lawyers in new positions, but that is a by-product and not the ultimate goal. Clearly, we owe duties to the prospective laterals with whom we work, mainly the duties of confidentiality and discretion, and the duty to disclose information relevant to prospective laterals' career decisions. But those in the legal community should understand that we work for the employers (the law firms and corporate legal departments) and not the prospective laterals.

The reason this distinction is important is because it explains our perspective as talent brokers. Legal talent brokers view the legal community through a very specific lens, and this lens is critically important to most members of the legal community because it provides the view of what the market wants.

Talent brokers do not determine the markets. We do not decide what a prospective lateral's rates need to be, what her book should be, or anything else. Our clients establish the criteria. They decide what they want in a lateral, they tell us, and then we go out and find the lawyers who meet those criteria and bring them to the table.

Why does this matter? Why is this critically important to much of the legal community? It is important because the criteria given to us, especially consistent criteria over an ongoing period of time, establishes the lateral attorney market. This creates the market. This tells the legal community what the market is seeking. Any lawyer who is interested in a lateral move, or even interested in what is going on in the legal community, needs to know what the market wants.

As talent brokers, we spend every single day learning what the market wants and then finding those who fit that description. Any lawyer who wants to know his value in the market, or whether his pay is in line with the market, or what his other options might be theoretically, will need to understand what the market conditions are. The best way to gain this knowledge is to start with a good legal talent broker.

Not only do good legal talent brokers have the most accurate, up-to-date information on the market, but we also have a unique view of the market itself. Unlike stockbrokers or real estate brokers, legal talent brokers deal with people. This is part of what makes our business fun. We work with some very interesting people, and some very challenging people. But they are people. They are people with real problems, real joys, real emotions, and real lives.

Nevertheless, from a business perspective, it is critical to view people objectively. Subjectivity can lead to poor decisions. As talent brokers, we have learned from experience that talent should be viewed as revenue-producing assets, similar to an operating machine. Obviously, we know people are not machines, and certainly we treat all people with whom we interact with respect and courtesy, but when it comes to making business decisions about legal talent, it is best to view legal talent as revenue-producing assets.

As with any other asset, the value is dependent upon production. Some assets are worth more than others on the open market. Some assets, while valuable, do not fit the needs of the entity in question. Viewed in this manner, and setting aside emotions to the maximum extent possible, law firm leaders will make better business decisions about what talent to acquire and what not to acquire. Our job as legal talent brokers is to help law firm leaders view talent from the proper business perspective and ultimately make the right decision based on objective criteria.

As a talent broker, my view of the overall market is that it has been and will remain an active, healthy market. Although it will fluctuate with the economy, and certain practice areas will be more in demand than others at specific times, the overall market for partner-level laterals is likely to remain consistent when viewed on a long-term basis.

The reason for my belief is that law firms will continue to want to grow to satisfy the needs of their clients. The demand for legal services continues to be strong. The overall demand will periodically decrease, but these decreases in demand will be cyclical. On a long-term basis, and considering all major practice areas in the aggregate, demand will remain strong.

Plus, as business entities, most law firms will of course want to grow rather than shrink, and businesses usually do one or the other. Maintaining the status quo on an ongoing basis is quite rare for businesses of a certain size.

In order to grow, law firms will have to add attorneys. That is really their only option. Whether by lateral hire, group acquisition, or law firm merger, law firms will have to add lawyers in order to grow. Organic growth will help, but that is a slow, long-term solution to a chronic issue. When clients have needs today, they are unlikely to wait years to have their needs addressed.

Demand for the seller's talents is high, which increases her value and drives up the cost to acquire her services. Lawyers who have the requisite client base, expertise, and hourly rate have options in the market, and the astute ones understand their advantage. I believe this advantage will remain for the foreseeable future.

CONCLUSION

IN THE INTRODUCTION TO THIS BOOK, WE LOOKED AT two similarly situated law firms. They were of a similar size with comparable revenues, profits, and headcount. After ten years, however, the firms had taken dramatically different paths. One was thriving with increased rates, higher attorney incomes, better clients, and a bright future. The other was stagnant with lower attorney incomes, fewer clients, reduced headcount, and an uncertain future. The question we posed was this: how do law firms and lawyers ensure they follow the path of the successful firm and not the other firm?

Presumably, after reading this book you know the answer: talent. Talent is the great differentiator in most human endeavors, and it is certainly the great differentiator among law firms.

The law firms that do the best job of filling their firm with the most talented lawyers will almost always enjoy the greatest success. That, of course, raises the question: how do you get this talent?

To answer that question, you must first understand what talent is. In the legal industry, talent is not simply innate skills and intelligence. Those are a part of it, of course, but only a part. Talent in the legal industry also includes work ethic, experience, legal skills, and the ability to bring in business. Stated differently, talent is best understood as a lawyer's overall value in the market.

In fact, the entire modern legal industry is based on this comprehensive definition of talent. It is this definition that gave rise to modern law firms with their ever-increasing size, scope, service offerings, revenues, profits, and incomes. These dramatic expansions did not happen until the market began to view and measure lawyers based on their overall value in the market, or in other words, their talent.

With our understanding of how the legal market views talent, the next obvious question for law firm leaders is this: how do we get this talent for our firm?

There are really only two ways to do so. The first is organic growth in which firms hire graduating law school students and train and develop them over a number of years. The other way is lateral hiring. Although some will point out that law firm mergers and group acquisitions are excellent ways to add talent, which is true, these are really other forms of lateral hiring. Whether by individual lateral hires or by group hires or law firm acquisitions, lateral hiring is a much faster, more efficient, and more profitable strategy for law firms to add needed talent compared to organic growth.

Just as your law firm probably has a number of reasons for wanting to add talent to its roster, individual attorneys have a number of reasons for exploring lateral moves. The most successful law firms understand these reasons and leverage them. Compensation, of course, is the primary reason lawyers make lateral moves, but higher compensation for lawyers is typically obtained through structural elements good law firms can provide, such as footprint, autonomy, management, and depth.

Furthermore, culture and camaraderie can be very important to prospective laterals.

If you are a law firm leader with responsibility for lateral hiring, or if you are a successful attorney considering your lateral options, it is critically important that you execute your role in the lateral process correctly. Firm leaders should remember the Lateral Candidate Experience as the perspective that truly matters in the lateral hiring process. Firms should avoid the common mistakes that frequently hinder law firms' recruiting efforts. Similarly, laterals should avoid the common mistakes that inhibit many lawyers' career trajectories. Too many promising careers have been upended because of mistakes that could have easily been avoided.

Both hiring law firm leaders and prospective laterals should, of course, be mindful of the ethical considerations in lateral hiring. Too many lawyers and law firms run afoul of these ethical principles because the firms and laterals are not familiar with them. There is too much at stake in a lateral hire to not learn these principles and follow them.

Furthermore, both hiring law firms and prospective laterals should always conduct proper due diligence before finalizing a lateral hire. A lateral hire is important. It is vitally important to the lateral's career, and it is a major investment by the hiring firm. Any decision this important must include sufficient due diligence as a part of the process.

Coming full circle, how do law firm leaders ensure their firms grow and thrive? How do prospective laterals make sure they transition to the law firms that will advance their practices and careers? How do you win the talent game? Follow the advice in this book, grow, and succeed.

ACKNOWLEDGMENTS

WRITING THIS BOOK FULFILLS A LIFELONG GOAL OF MINE. As with any goal, achieving it was only possible because of the help I have received from many people along the way.

First and foremost, I would like to thank my wife, Heather. They say you will marry your best friend if you are very lucky. I did, and I am.

I would also like to thank:

My children, Laine and Richard, Jr. I am immensely proud of you both.

My mother, Louise Brock McCarron. In addition to being a great mom, you have been my lifelong supporter, advisor, and confidante.

My siblings, Paul Brock, Jr., Bette Rutan, Valerie Guiles, and Sherry McGowin. You have all been loving and supportive of me. I have been fortunate to be the youngest.

My team at OnBoard. You all are the best colleagues I have ever had.

Brad Hawley for, among many other things, intentionally or unintentionally motivating me to write this book.

Joe Freedman for, among many other things, giving me my start in this industry.

DeAnn Amason, for keeping things straight with skill and integrity.

Kevin Fisher, for helping me become a better leader.

Duncan Hulsey, for being a good partner in a passion project.

Tina Solis, for expertise and guidance on the ethical issues involved in lateral hiring.

For my true friends (you know who you are), for keeping me laughing, grounded, and motivated.

Finally, I would like to thank Sophie May and everyone at Scribe who made this process much easier in countless ways.

www.ingramcontent.com/pod-product-compliance
Lightning Source LLC
Chambersburg PA
CBHW031853200326
41597CB00012B/391